TRAVELLERS' MONEY

TRAVELLERS' MONEY

JOHN BOOKER

ALAN SUTTON PUBLISHING LIMITED

First published in the United Kingdom in 1994
Alan Sutton Publishing Limited
Phoenix Mill · Far Thrupp · Stroud · Gloucestershire

First published in the United States of America in 1994
Alan Sutton Publishing Inc
83 Washington Street · Dover · NH 03820

British Library Cataloguing-in-Publication Data

A catalogue record for this book is available from the British Library.

ISBN 0 7509 0597 2

Library of Congress Cataloging-in-Publication Data applied for

The publication of this book has
been made possible by a generous
grant from Lloyds Bank Plc

Typeset in 10/12 Bembo.
Typesetting and origination by
Alan Sutton Publishing Limited.
Printed in Great Britain by
The Bath Press, Avon

CONTENTS

ACKNOWLEDGEMENTS

It is my happy duty to acknowledge the assistance of many friends and colleagues in banking and archival centres. My main debt of gratitude is to my employer, Lloyds Bank, which has underwritten publication costs to a most welcome and significant extent. The generous support and interest of many senior figures in the bank echoes the key role which the company's archives have played in unfolding the story in these pages. Within my own section this project evolved many years ago in the form of an archive teaching kit, in which my predecessor Mr M.D. Roberts was enthusiastically involved. In other institutions I am indebted to Mrs Barbara Peters, Archivist, Coutts & Co.; Mr Henry Gillett and Mr John Keyworth of the Bank of England Archives and Museum Services respectively; Mrs Jean Farrugia and Mr Peter Howe, of the Post Office Archives and Public Relations Department respectively; Mr I.F. Wright, Departmental Records Officer, HM Customs & Excise; Mr Howard Morgan, Vice-President and General Manager, Financial Services Institutions, American Express Europe Limited; and to the Thomas Cook Archives and Library which produces many interesting and useful publications. Finally, it is a particular pleasure to pay tribute to the resources of the British Library, the London Library, and the Guildhall Library, and the helpful guidance of their staff. In the text which has resulted, all errors, omissions and opinions are of course my own responsibility.

Illustrations are all taken from material in the ownership of Lloyds Bank or myself, with the exception of those on p. 48, reproduced by permission of the British Library, and p. 93, reproduced by courtesy of The Post Office. I am also grateful to John Murray (Publishers) Ltd for permission to quote extracts from Leslie A. Marchand (ed.), *Byron's Letters and Journals 1816–1823*, 12 vols (London 1973–82), and to The University of Michigan Press for permission to quote extracts from H. Barrows (ed.), *Observations and Reflections Made in the Course of a Journey Through France, Italy, and Germany by Hester Lynch Piozzi* (Ann Arbor, 1967), copyright of the University of Michigan, 1967.

Finally, the illustration on p. 92 is taken from H. Robinson, *Britain's Post Office* (Oxford, 1953), p. 113. I have been unable to trace Professor Howard to grant me permission to reproduce this. I therefore beg the indulgence of the copyright holder for any infringement.

John Booker
January 1994

INTRODUCTION

Travel books have been so abundant over the last four centuries that all the tips and tales form a heady concoction of knowledge – a kind of rich and enticing punch from which all are welcome to draw. Each log of a journey, every impression of a foreign land adds a little grain of spice to the mixture. The effect, on those who drink deeply, can be very potent. Geographers, for instance, dizzy themselves on references to crossings, mountains, routes and towns; even social historians can get quite merry from tourists' impressions of foreign hosts and their manners.

There is, however, one branch of the history of travel which has been largely overlooked, perhaps because it straddles a kind of no-man's-land between banking and tourism. This neglected area is the provision of travellers' money, more especially in the form of credit.

A distinction must immediately be made between comment and experience. Tourists' comment, that is advice to other intending tourists about foreign money, has never been hard to find. From the seventeenth century, travellers are told how to carry it, hide it and spend it, and are guided with a greater or lesser degree of clarity through the dreadful mess of European coinage systems. There is even some advice about monetary preparation before setting off; this is not so frequent, alas, in the nineteenth century, as guidance on getting a passport, but certainly enough to show how the provision of some kind of paper credit was always a sensible and practical alternative to carrying specie (i.e. gold and silver coins).

The real gap in knowledge is about first-hand experiences: the factual and anecdotal record of how early tourists and travellers got by with their merchant's paper and promises to pay. Only the minutest examination of countless journeys produces any information; and only the most patient analysis of the results reveals any sort of pattern. One reason for reticence might be that arrangements for foreign credit, for instance on the Grand Tour, were so well known that there seemed little point in explaining them. We are familiar with this attitude today.

The antiquity of the principle of the traveller's cheque has long been forgotten. Some people understand, quite rightly, that the American Express Company introduced the name, if not the spelling; others, perhaps, speculate that Thomas Cook had something to do with it. The fact is that the idea itself has been around for more than 230 years. The document was traditionally called a circular note and its introduction was rooted in the Grand Tour.

How and why the circular note was developed, and all related aspects of travellers' money supply before and after, are the substance of this book. By good fortune, many of the papers which explain the reasons behind the note, and how it was intended to work, have survived in the archives of Lloyds Bank, inherited from Herries, Farquhar & Co., a private firm of bankers at 16 St James's Street, London, absorbed in 1893.

These archives, precious and invaluable as they are, do not give the story its full dimension. For this breadth of view, enquiry must be made from the user's angle and from a wider documentation. Foreigners' experiences in Britain are as relevant as the experiences of the British abroad, as credit for incoming tourists was also a matter to be regularized in the late eighteenth century. Also examined are more utilitarian aspects of travel, such as passports and customs control, very much inter-linked, and by no means irrelevant to money supply.

The whole story has unravelled with a surprising result. A prototype travel agent has emerged whose helpfulness was taken for granted. The demands on his generosity and the scope of his obligation to foreign travellers, especially on the Continent, were without limit. This man was the banker, who left his office in Frankfurt or Geneva in the evening to fulfil a social duty to total strangers which was so relentless and overwhelming that his day-job in the counting-house must often have seemed tranquillity itself.

This book also charts the later development of travellers' money supply into current times. Perhaps readers of this book, next time they go abroad with traveller's cheques, could spare a thought for the memory of a man called Robert Herries who introduced the circular note and so becomes in a sense the hero of this narrative. Like so many innovators, Herries did not receive at the time the recognition he deserved, and he is still a forgotten visionary.

1
TRADE BEFORE TRAVEL: THE GROWTH OF MONEY AND BANKING

To travel in foreign parts is a natural instinct of mankind and the opportunity has usually been available. Most reasons for travel were traditionally rooted in business, diplomacy, religion or compulsion, and the point when travellers set out from less weighty motives is elusive. Even an 'official' journey could sometimes be turned into something more inwardly satisfying. No doubt every boatload of pilgrims sailing for Jerusalem or Spain in the Middle Ages had its quota of passengers whose piety took second place to a craving for adventure.

Yet even those whose motives for travel rested largely on personal curiosity had a sense of purpose or self-instruction which characterized their plans – educational in the context of the Grand Tour, adventurous and explorative in journeys through India, Russia and the Levant. This book considers all travellers whose motives were outside the realms of commerce or duty; in other words, those who journeyed because they wanted to and whose gain was not in a material sense but in the satisfaction of an impulse to experience and understand. It also considers those who, in more recent years, have travelled purely for recreation.

The common denominator among all travellers has always been the need for money. But if the facilities available are examined back through past centuries, the convenience and suitability of money and credit for the uncommercial traveller are seen to diminish progressively. Four centuries ago he was not recognized as an emerging species and no provision was made for his needs. To understand how the traveller adapted to this unproviding world, and then won his own provision, it is first necessary to consider the monetary framework of the period in which he lived.

In a primitive society there was no commercial necessity for money to exist. Trade by swapping or barter was an acceptable way of business, the item of exchange being whatever one party needed in return for its own product. Even when a coinage existed, it was possible to trade without it: in the eighteenth century, silk was still being bartered for cloth in Syria, while the Fine Arts trade among Russian nobility was supported by exchange. Money arose to provide some yardstick against which the relative value of bartered goods might be measured. This 'money' did not need to be metallic. In Homer's *Iliad* arms worth one hundred oxen are exchanged for bronze worth nine. However, metal was a better yardstick because it could also be used as the medium of exchange: it was portable and divisible, and the most durable metals, like gold and silver, were also the rarest, which was an additional advantage.

The awesome status of gold is now so prevalent that tales of its rejection, as late as the nineteenth century, seem almost unbelievable. Yet J. Frith, a round-the-world voyager in 1857–60, sailed near a remote Pacific island where the captain of his ship exchanged 'a yard of calico, rotten with damp and age' for what the inhabitants (who had salvaged the cargo of a wrecked Californian gold ship) took to be useless pieces of yellow metal: 'and when the exchange was made, the shrewd native laughed outright at . . . having so completely overreached him [the captain] in the bargain!'[1]

Once metallic money was introduced as a circulating medium, it was an obvious step for rulers to mark it in such a way as to identify ownership and value. Unfortunately, with natural abrasion, and given the intrinsic value of rare metal for other uses, coinage was open to misappropriation and downright mischief. The former amounted almost to a process of natural selection, known in monetary history as Gresham's Law. It was the theory of Sir Thomas Gresham (*c.* 1519–79), founder of London's Royal Exchange, that if two coins of the same type are in circulation, the one in better condition will be retained while the worse will be passed on; so that, eventually, only damaged coins will be in circulation while those of full weight will be hoarded, melted down for bullion or jewellery, or traded as merchandise.

The deliberate maltreatment of coinage was caused by 'sweating' (rubbing) or clipping, which reduced the weight and therefore the intrinsic worth, while those who debased the money in this way acquired small quantities of bullion. Sometimes money was adulterated even by those who issued it. Small states, particularly in Germany, often added metal baser than the coinage was supposed to contain; or imprinted arbitrary values, making the money pass at many times more than its intrinsic worth. In receiving light money the traveller was no more disadvantaged than anyone else, as long as he took care to spend it in the country of origin. Only by bad luck was he involved in the really serious problems arising from money which was illegally minted or counterfeit.

The former problem was brought home to Dr Charles Maclean in Paris in 1802. An Englishman, whom he had once treated in Germany, wrote to him from the gaol of the Conciergerie requesting a visit. Maclean broke through the bureaucratic curtain to reach him. The unfortunate prisoner had bought 300 louis d'ors from a reputable money-changer in Hamburg. The coins were new, and of full weight, but had been minted outside France. When the traveller presented them in all innocence to a Parisian banker, he was arrested and imprisoned for three months. This harsh treatment seemed anti-British. Maclean noted that a German citizen, and a legate of the Pope, had both been detected with similar illegal money but neither had been arrested.[2]

A country on the tourist circuit which suffered particularly from counterfeit money was Turkey. Its indigenous gold coin, based on the Venetian sequin, was rare, and most local money consisted of the para and piastre, low denomination coins no match for the silver currencies of western Europe. Imitations of these coins, low in silver, were often minted unlawfully for the Turkish market. Another problem was the simmering antagonism between Turkey and Greece, the latter forming part of the European province of Turkey until the rebellion of 1829. Some twenty or thirty small mints were set up at Hydra and Spezzia, islands off the south of Greece (an area then known as Morea), deliberately to copy and debase Turkish money and weaken the country's economy.

Penalties for passing such money were horrific and Turkish justice was immediate. An English visitor to Smyrna in 1829 came across a crowd of children, near the bazaar, gathered round a corpse. The headless body was that of a Greek, caught passing counterfeit money and executed there and then to the delight of the street urchins: 'they kept screaming, and chattering and touching him with their feet, till one, having smeared the face of another with a stick dipped in the blood, . . . flew off convulsed with laughter to the Bazaar, where he was followed by the whole party in full cry, who seemed marvellously delighted with the exploit'. This was small comfort to the tourist, who might not know the validity of the coin in his pocket.[3]

Certain European currencies were, by reason of trade or colonization, in demand in areas far removed from their point of origin. Dutch money was traditionally good tender in Sweden and provided the only gold and silver coinage in late eighteenth century Russia. French money held sway as far as the Rhine and could not be dislodged from Poland when a

A Smyrna bazaar. Grand Tourists who went as far as Smyrna risked immediate execution if they tendered counterfeit money

kingdom was formed there in 1815 under the emperor of Russia. The people's allegiance was still to Napoleon who, in 1807, had united a great part of the ancient country into the Grand Duchy of Warsaw. The English traveller C.E. Dod met a Polish officer in Germany in 1820: 'He had lately come from Warsaw, where he said, the French were regretted beyond measure – that the Russians and Poles were fighting daily in the streets – the French was almost the only coin that tradesmen would accept.'[4]

The Spanish silver dollar (the fabled piece-of-eight) formed most of the bullion in the Bank of Hamburg, dominated the West Indies and South America, and was strong in the near East. The British-run Levant Company brought in nearly £20,000 worth of Dutch and Spanish dollars in 1690, while individual traders there imported Spanish bullion under the paperwork name of 'hard lemons'.[5] Shipment of specie out of Spain was always illegal: in 1605 an English ship in San Sebastian had been ransacked and nearly wrecked on the false rumour that it held 15,000 ducats being smuggled abroad. There was no redress for the damage.[6]

In the Far East, dependence on other countries' money was equally strong. The fledgling Australian government, in 1813, imported 40,000 Spanish dollars as a source of bullion. The middles were punched out and so two coins were created: the outer rings circulated by the name of 'holeys', given a value of 5s, and the inner circles were known as 'dumps', worth 1s 3d. These denominations were more than the intrinsic value of the silver.[7]

While countries with an inadequate native coinage or a colonial overlord might be happy with other people's money, the scene within Europe was bedevilled by jealous self-interest. The worst experiences for travellers were in the small states of Germany and Italy. Warnings had been sounded by Fynes Moryson in the early seventeenth century and were repeated by Thomas Nugent in his Georgian treatise on the Grand Tour. But the information in depth which they sought to provide was so defeatingly complex that the traveller was no better off. Even a century later the position had barely improved. Warnings about Germany, like the following by the Scotsman J. Aiton, continued the catalogue of differences while seeking to explain the problem:

> There are so very many different states . . . some of them not so extensive as our Scottish counties; these are governed by dukes, or princes, or petty sovereigns, some of whom are as poor and proud as our Highland chieftans were wont to be previous to the last rebellion.

Each of these must . . . see his own pretty face on the coins of his own country . . . there is convention money and shein gold, and good groschens, and silver groschens, and florins, and francs, and stivers, and gilders, and kreutzers, and cents, and zwanzigers, and marks, and thalers, and kron thalers, and Saxon thalers, and nominal thalers, and convention, or species thalers, and many others whose names   were   never   learned,   or   are   now   forgotten . . . at length you begin to acquire something like a knowledge of the names and value of some of these coins . . . but by this time you have crossed the frontier. . . there are in your pockets now perhaps five or six shillings worth of small coin, of no intrinsic value, and which is not current in the house where you are now, because you have crossed a clumsy wooden bridge some two or three hours before.[8]

The real point about German money was that it existed at different levels and only the so-called 'convention' money (that is, money agreed by convention) gained inter-state acceptance. In the German provinces of Austria, for instance, there were two sorts of coin in circulation: convention money (*güten-munze*) and coarse (*schein*) money, both denominated by gulden (florins). The former were worth twice the latter. While money was generally counted in *schein* gulden, the risk for the unwary traveller was that he might pay in *güten-munze* and the hotelier or shopkeeper might not be honest enough to correct him. In some Bavarian towns, like Ratisbon, the distinction was between 'white' money for everyday use and 'black' money by which rates and taxes were paid. At nearby Augsburg there were three kinds of money: exchange money, for bills of exchange, worth 27 per cent more than the second tier, convention money; while the third tier, local white money, lost 20 per cent against convention money and 52 per cent against exchange money.[9]

Such differing levels of money were by no means confined to Germany, and the reason can be traced back to the breakdown of the silver coinages, summarized as denarii, which had been ubiquitous in western Europe until the thirteenth century. From this Latin word came the English 'penny', the German 'pfennig', the French 'denier', the Spanish 'dinero' and so on. (In fact, much of Europe once had a pound, shillings and pence currency, with 12 pence to a shilling and 20 shillings to a pound, so what we remember as a uniquely British system was very much continental in origin.) As types of denarius became increasingly debased, and as suspect indigenous coinages were introduced alongside them, so the need arose for a bookkeeping 'money of account', sometimes called 'banco', to represent intrinsic worth. While money of account acted as a measure of value, everyday money was used as a medium of exchange. The former is often referred to in old travel books as 'imaginary' money. The Bank of Hamburg, for instance, operated on the basis of a coin called the mark-banco, which did not exist, while the city's merchants made payments in real marks, worth some 20 per cent less.[10] An example in England of money of account was the pound sterling: such a coin was not found and its value was made manifest by the gold sovereign.

The same problems of defective local currencies led to the trade between nations being conducted on the notion of mint par of exchange, rather than the value of cash in hand. Mint par is the intrinsic value or mint weight of one coinage expressed in terms of another. This principle, however, did nothing for the problem of money transmission, where both the weight of specie and the danger of robbery posed problems for the settlement of international debts. The solution, adopted in western Europe by the end of the thirteenth century, was the bill of exchange[11] – an instrument by no means absent from the traveller's portfolio, as will be seen in the next chapter.

There were sometimes four parties to a bill of exchange, and the procedure was as follows. A merchant in, say, Genoa, wishing to send money abroad, say to Lyons, deposited the amount with a local intermediary, usually a banker, who gave in return a bill upon his Lyons correspondent. The bill was sent by the merchant to the party he intended to pay, who presented it to the Lyons correspondent of the Genoa banker, who paid him. The debt was now a matter between bankers.

Later it was quite normal to have only two parties to a bill of exchange, particularly in local, routine business between mercantile houses. Thus the bill was virtually, in our terms, a cheque, with an in-built facility for credit. The party who drew up the bill (who was also the party to be paid) was known as the drawer; the party who signed the bill and thereby agreed to pay, was known as the acceptor. He returned the bill to the drawer until payment was due. All bills of exchange carried the words 'value received', signifying that the acceptor had received goods worth the sum he was undertaking to pay.

Owing to the uncertainties of despatch, long-distance bills were forwarded in triplicate ('thirds of exchange') and payment was due against any one copy. It was possible for local bills to be settled 'at sight' but most, and all international bills, allowed a long period before payment, partly to absorb travelling time. This period of currency was known as 'usance' and was often one month, but could be three, for instance between London and Venice, and sometimes even longer. Payment could also be at half usance or double usance. Between Java and England bills were drawn at six months' sight, and as the journey time was two months an importer had effectively eight months' credit – more than enough time in which to raise money by organizing the sale of the cargo.[12]

It follows that in any transaction by bill of exchange the drawer might have to wait a long time for his money. But if the bill was back in his possession, he could take it to a banker who would buy it for rather less than its face value, a process known as discounting. Thereby, the drawer had a sum approaching full payment before maturity of the bill, while the banker received the whole sum from the acceptor at the end of usance.

Bankers and merchants did all they could to avoid an imbalance of trade because deficiencies had ultimately to be made up by the transfer of bullion. Sometimes merchants bought bills from one another to square their own books, while people like tax collectors, who had money to remit to a central treasury, paid cash for bills drawn on the place where their money was destined. As long as the bills were good, there was then no need to send ready money on a perilous journey. By the sixteenth century, the annual fair at Lyons was an occasion for French merchants to

Bullion arriving by steam lorry at Calcutta Mint in around 1910

The English had a reputation for informality in the handling of bullion. In these Edwardian photographs, workmen and porters (with just a sprinkling of police among the latter) pose with silver ingots in London's dockland, and at Euston station gather for a general settlement of debts, using bills of exchange which had passed from hand to hand by endorsement and thus acquired something of the status of banknotes.[13]

In international trade, imbalances could be counteracted to some extent by an adjustment of the exchange rate, but again the movement of bullion or specie was the ultimate resort. In the late eighteenth century, the emperor of Germany, already subsidized by England, borrowed heavily from the Bank of Hamburg, repaying by bills on England for merchandise. Fast schooners were kept solely to move bullion between Hamburg and London, the exchange rate being so volatile that a vessel might go straight back with the money it had just brought over in the opposite direction.[14]

Shipments of bullion did not, of course, affect the traveller but he could be pleased or disappointed, as today, by movements in the exchange rate. Before the French Revolution, for example, the English guinea and the louis d'or (24 livres) were at par. In 1792 the guinea fetched 44 livres and English families resident in France drew bills on London and so all but doubled their income. Some countries, like Poland, had no recognized course of exchange with any trading place in Europe, and in others it was limited. Copenhagen had an exchange rate based only on Hamburg, Amsterdam and London, while in Russia the exchange was based solely on Holland. The rouble, worth 100 Dutch sous in the early eighteenth century, sank as low as 27 sous in 1790. This meant that Russian people living abroad on government business had to be paid at a fixed rate of 50 sous to the rouble to make ends meet – an example which the French traveller, Fortia de Piles, suggested might have a wider international appeal: consuls of his own country received only 2 or 3 louis d'ors instead of the pre-Revolution 100, and were in danger of dishonouring their fellow countrymen (the 'premier race of the world') by starving to death.[15]

The letter of credit was another instrument used between bankers and merchants. This document was an authority to the addressee to allow a named third party (the bearer) to draw on demand up to a specifed sum, charging to the account of the grantor. It could be used at the same time to commend the bearer to the kind attentions of the addressee and so it became, as will be seen, a more useful document for the traveller than the bill of exchange. A disadvantage of letters of credit, as compared with bills, in business terms was that they lacked their legal muscle: without the magic words 'value received', the case for redress was weaker if letters were dishonoured. The Alsatian traveller J.E. Zetzner, who later became a banker, had exactly this problem in 1701.[16] Wishing to go to Norway to set up in business, he got a respectable Strasbourg chemist, called

Spielmann, to give him a letter of credit for 1,500 florins, drawn on a banker in Amsterdam. But the banker refused to pay the money until he himself had received it from Spielmann. Thus Zetzner had the expense of a wasted journey to Holland and no money when he got there. The experiences of English travellers with letters of credit were apparently very much better.

The form of paper money most common today is of course the banknote, which has a fascinating history of evolution from well before the days of the Grand Tour, and one which is by no means confined to the Italian city states, or even to Europe. As the issuing bank promises to pay the bearer on demand, the banknote is technically a promissory note, although there can be types of promissory note which involve payment after notice, and in that case the document approaches close to a bill of exchange. What the banker promises to pay in his banknote is specie to the face value of the note. It has rarely been the case that any country or bank has had enough bullion alone to cover its paper money, and notes have generally been issued partly against government or other good securities. In 1797, during the French wars, the Bank of England was prevented by government from repaying its banknotes with gold, a suspension which lasted twenty-four years.[17] By the Gold Standard Act, 1925, the obligation of the Bank of England to pay legal coin for its note issue was removed absolutely.

In mainland Europe, the evolution of banknotes was chaotic. Zetzner recorded that during the War of the Spanish Succession (1702–14), the value of '*les billets de monnaye*' rose or fell 10 to 15 per cent from one post to the next, making a fortune for some merchants and ruining others. By 1709 paper money was in such disfavour 'that those who had to make payments and had nothing else in hand but these unfortunate notes, were forced to pay ten thousand pounds when they had a debt of one thousand pounds, while they had to accept these notes at their face value'.[18]

English travellers in Rome in the mid-eighteenth century found paper money universal. Lady Mary Wortley Montagu, in 1740, received 50 sequins from the banker Belloni 'which he solemnly swore was all the money he had in the house. They go to market with paper, pay the lodgings with paper, and, in short, there is no specie to be seen, which raises the price of everything to the utmost extravagance, nobody knowing what to ask for their goods.'[19] Some twenty-five years later, nothing had changed. Smollett noted that gold and silver barely existed 'and the very bankers, on whom strangers have their credit, make interest to pay their tradesmen's bills with paper notes on the bank of Spirito

Santo'.[20] Another bad period for notes, at least in France, was during the Revolution, when the government issued the infamous assignats – paper money secured on confiscated land. The issue depreciated rapidly in value, not least against sterling.

In the north of Europe, paper money was especially in favour. In Denmark banknotes were ubiquitous, and also safe, because the national bank was obliged to hold specie to secure the issue. Nathaniel Wraxall reported from Copenhagen in 1774 that he had seen no gold and hardly any silver. 'They pay every thing in paper; and if you lose a single dollar at the card-table, or the billiard-table, it is given in a bill, or note. I received two hundred rix-dollars yesterday morning, and not a single one in money.'[21] Sweden was similar. Fortia de Piles had recourse to six people, including the postmaster, to break down a bank-note into smaller notes, and he still needed copper coins for tipping his postilion.[22]

Less credit-worthy were the eighteenth century banknotes of Russia. The bank at St Petersburg, owned by the Crown and housed in purpose-built premises designed by Quarenghi, issued paper to a greater value than the coin which supported it. This coinage was of copper and arrived ready-minted by boat from Siberia.[23] Each shipment, carried in massive barrels, was worth around 80,000 roubles. The coins were carried into fifty-six identical store-rooms where the money was counted out into bags, each of the value of 5 roubles. Banknotes circulated in denominations of 100, 50, 25, 10 and 5 roubles. People wishing to break down the larger notes could call at the bank and exchange them for lower value notes and 5-rouble bags of copper. About two million copper roubles were distributed in this way in a year, whereas notes in circulation ran to twelve or thirteen times that value. Fortia de Piles found this system weak but not ungenerous, as in some countries no real money was ever given: 'le papier russe n'est pas encore le plus mauvais de l'Europe'.[24]

The lack of gold and silver in Russia led to some ingenious substitution for ready money. In St Petersburg the explorer Edward Clarke was told of a British physician who, in return for his professional services to a nobleman, regularly received a snuff-box 'and as regularly carried it to a jeweller for sale. The jeweller sold it again to the . . . nobleman who wanted a fee for his physician, so that the doctor obtained his box again; and at last the matter became so well understood between the jeweller and the physician, that it was considered by both parties as a sort of bank-note, and no words were necessary in transacting the sale of it.'[25]

By the nineteenth century, banknotes were quite universal and held in less mistrust by travellers, although guidebooks warned of forgeries and advised against too large a stock. Turkey had an unusual form of banknote called sehhim, introduced in 1840 and denominated by 25, 50 and 100 piastres.[26] These bore interest at 12½ per cent per annum and were therefore closer to treasury bonds. Sometimes they were low in value and could scarcely be passed at all in the bazaars; but at other times, especially when interest payments were due, they were at a premium both as money and as a marketable commodity. There were, however, other drawbacks to sehhim: the Turkish government paid all its salaries in specie, which lessened the credibility of paper in the eyes of the tourist, and the notes themselves were of poor quality. Unfortunately, this was the case with much non-European money. A visitor to Java in 1857 found the paper money both of government and the local private bank to be 'a miserable trashy stuff', soon to be abandoned altogether in favour of coin.[27]

Some reference has already been made to the powerful national and civic banks which governed the growth of the European economy. Many others might be mentioned, like the Bank of Amsterdam founded in 1609. The operation of this bank, in many respects the Bank of Holland, was based on the Venetian Banco del Giro, but without the facility for lending to government in time of war. But such banks had no more relevance to the tourist than the national banks have today. Furthermore, the number of English travellers who tried to visit central banks, against appropriate letters of introduction, was minimal. This is curious because the Bank of England, founded in 1694, was very much a stop on the foreign tourist's visit to London. However, there was much curiosity about exchanges (notably at Bordeaux) and about mints, which were regularly visited not only in large towns, for instance Milan and Stockholm, but also at mining centres like Cremnitz in Hungary, and even in developing countries such as India. The American traveller George F. Train has left a vivid description of the Calcutta mint in 1856, where 'the device of the East India Company, the value of the coin, the date of the die, and the profile of her most gracious Majesty' were impressed on rupees in a temperature so intolerable that black men turned white and died young.[28]

The level of banking which interested the traveller, then as now, was essentially that at which he could realize or exchange his money. Although the existence of private banks was by no means restricted to England, the profession abroad lacked structure and definition. Under the umbrella of banking sheltered (or lurked) money-changers and money-lenders of greater or lesser respectability. Money changers were important for travellers, especially when crossing the petty dukedoms of Germany,

Calcutta, with views of Government House, the Town Hall and Treasury. The Mint, which supplied the Treasury with its coinage, was about a mile away, on the banks of the River Hooghly

and some, like Meyer Amschel Rothschild of Frankfurt, rose to great prosperity. Other men turned to money-changing as a logical extension of their main business. The classic example was Monsieur Dessein, owner of a hotel at Calais in the late eighteenth century, who, according to Philip Thicknesse, made around £50,000 by changing money for the English tourist.[29] In Germany postmasters acted as money changers, much to the chagrin of Dr Rigby, who dismissed them as rascals.[30] Generally any innkeeper and even some shopkeepers on the Continent were prepared to exchange specie at something close to the formal exchange rate.

Only *in extremis* would a traveller become involved with money-lenders, who had a particularly bad press on account of the Christian aversion to usury. But through literary, as distinct from historical, writing it has become impossible to distinguish them from the more complicated mainstream of the banking profession. An extract from a letter of the poet Shelley illustrates the difficulty. Travelling through north Italy in 1818, Shelley stopped at a property near Ferrara: 'I ought to say', he reported, 'that one of the farms belongs to a Jewish banker at Venice, another Shylock.'[31] But Shylock had not been a banker: Shakespeare portrays him as a money-lender. Confusion arose not simply because the jobs were related but because the race which combined these and so many other monetary activities was the Jewish race (as Shelley of course realized) and Christendom was as dismissive of their business as of their culture.

The nature of this intolerance varied across Europe, to some extent polarizing on an east–west axis. Conditions for the Jews were best in Muslim Turkey. Lady Mary Wortley Montagu, at Adrianople in 1717, found 'most of the rich tradesmen were Jews. That people are in incredible power in this country. They have many privileges above all the natural Turks themselves . . . and have drawn the whole trade of the empire into their hands. . . . Every pasha has his Jew, who is his *homme d'affaires*. . . .'[32] A visitor to Turkey in 1829 also found the Jews a favoured people there. The Turks described them as 'visitors' whereas Greeks were called 'slaves' and Armenians 'subjects'. The same traveller was equally impressed in Christian Hungary, where, in the great entrepôt of Arad, he found Jews 'being allowed exclusive monopolies of tobacco, corn, and other commodities by which they have amassed immense wealth'.[33]

In Germany, however, it was a quite different story: among the cities of Saxony, Jews were tolerated only in Dresden and Leipzig but had no rights of citizenship; in Bremen and elsewhere they could not even spend a night without payment of a large fine; and in cities which accepted them they were forced to live in defined areas and subjected to humiliating duties. The most important German ghetto (to use the Venetian term) was at Frankfurt. In this city it was said 'the Roman Catholics have the churches, the Lutherans the magistrates, and the Calvinists the money'.[34] In fact, there was considerable wealth also in the ghetto, which had around 12 per cent of the city's population, but in social terms the conditions were unspeakable. The ghetto was a single street, gated at night, where, as Dr Moore observed in the 1770s, the inhabitants were cooped together until morning 'like so many black cattle'.[35] When they were allowed out in the day, it was against irksome restrictions and duties, one of which was to carry water for fire-fighting. This environment was the cradle of the Rothschilds.

Britain was in the forefront of anti-Jewish feeling. Englishmen of the Renaissance, living in a country from where all Jews had been expelled in 1290, appear to have imbibed anti-semitism with their mother's milk. Fynes Moryson, a decent and well-educated man, referred to Jews at Frankfurt who 'sucke the blood of Christians by extortion',[36] while Shakespeare's *Merchant of Venice*, drawing to some extent from Christopher Marlowe's earlier play *The Jew of Malta*, imagined an irreconcilable conflict of ideologies where the Jewish money-lender sought revenge for his treatment by Antonio at the Rialto exchange:

> Signior Antonio, many a time and oft
> In the Rialto you have rated me
> About my money and my usances.
> Still have I borne it with a patient shrug,
> For sufferance is the badge of all our tribe.
> You call me misbeliever, cut-throat dog,
> And spit upon my Jewish gaberdine . . . [37]

Doctrinal problems aside, the reputation of Jews for sharp practice was another main reason why they were disliked. While some of this ill-will was rooted in jealousy of their flair for business, the literature of travel does give allegations, if not proof, of undesirable behaviour. In Germany Thomas Nugent accused them of clipping coins while Dr Beattie told of a self-styled Irishman, passing off English sovereigns as guineas, who was unmasked as a Livonian Jew.[38] Fortia de Piles found them running a highly illegal and profitable business selling Danish specie in Hamburg.[39] J. Frith, recounting his round-the-world voyage in the late 1850s, blamed Jews for his worst experiences: 'I had escaped the Ceylon elephants, Indian sepoys, and Chinese braves, all but the children of Esau and Ishmael, who, whilst with other travellers I was crossing a bridge of boats over the Nile, cut my waistcoat into shreds, for the charitable purpose of relieving me of the burthen of my sovereigns in the inside pocket.'[40] Another mid-Victorian traveller, Charles Terry, found himself on board ship with a Jewish money lender who was pursuing a debtor from Jerusalem to Calcutta. Generally a 'meek' man, the Jew when asked a wrong question 'was instantly fired with rage, his countenance was hideous, his bleared eyes gazed daggers. . . . Shakespeare, one would think, must have seen some such creature as this, ere he depicted his Shylock'.[41]

Other travellers told fearsome stories about interest rates. Peter Beckford, brother of the more famous William, reporting from Siena in 1805, heard that when a Jew had no good security, interest on a loan of 400 crowns was 10 per cent a month.[42] In Germany Dr Beattie was told of 70 crowns to be repaid in a month by 100.[43] In Greece, George Cochrane was astonished to find his landlady's brother asking him for a 200 dollar loan at 40 per cent interest. 'He said that he had been to a Jew money-lender that morning, who had offered to let him have the money at sixty per cent. I asked this man if it was usual to give forty per cent. He said that thirty was very common, but that forty was often given where the party much wanted the money.'[44]

The importance of this overt or latent anti-Semitism in the wider context of travel is that Jewish bankers, even the most prosperous, were excluded from the coterie of correspondent firms to whom English tourists were recommended by their domestic bankers. Following chapters will show the extraordinary lengths to which the social obligations of these correspondent links sometimes extended. The Englishman abroad used Jewish bankers and money-lenders only when he had no pre-arranged facility with a Christian banker – that is to say, when he varied his route as he went along or needed to exchange specie from one country to another. In such dealings with professional Jewish bankers there is minimal evidence that travellers were dissatisfied with the service. Certainly it was irksome to find offices closed on Saturdays, but no more so than finding them closed for other religious reasons, like a 'morose' Calvinist festival in Geneva.[45]

Many European bankers, both Jewish and Christian, established great wealth and influence. Prince Pückler-Muskau was especially in awe of the Rothschild dynasty 'without whom no power in Europe today [1828] seems able to make war'.[46] But, for the reasons already given, there was no social intercourse at Frankfurt between the Rothschilds and the English Grand Tourist. The affluence (if not the influence) of many Christian bankers was equally fabled. Again Frankfurt was in the forefront, where many generations of the von Bethmann family lived and spent like royalty. To reach this social position had not been easy. In the 1770s Dr John

Frankfurt-on-Main, showing the town hall (Römer). Frankfurt, the most commercially important of the southern German cities, became a cultural centre, thanks to the generosity of its bankers, notably Städel and von Bethmann. It was also the cradle of the Rothschild dynasty, whose business began in the city's Jewish quarter

Moore, the social commentator, still found a strong division between the local nobility and the bourgeoisie. The latter, who included bankers, had:

> by commerce, or some profession equally ignoble, attained great wealth, which enables them to live in a style of magnificence unbecoming their rank; yet their noble neighbours insinuate, that they always retain a vulgarity of sentiment and manners, unknown to those whose blood has flowed pure through several generations, unmixed with that puddle which stagnates in the veins of plebeians.[47]

By the 1820s, however, the banker Moritz von Bethmann was known as 'the king of Frankfurt'. This position was achieved by patronage of the fine arts and a careful manipulation of society. Charles Dod noted that Frankfurt bankers had become 'convenient friends for their Diplomatists; and their smart wives and daughters, no disagreeable resources to the young nobles who study diplomacy in the ambassador's bureaux. A gay young Count, attached to a legation, is the acknowledged *cavaliere servente* [lover] of a pretty banker's wife. . . .'[48] As for the fine arts, the banker Städel gave a million florins for the foundation of an art gallery and the support of young artists: 'there is scarcely a merchant or banker in Frankfort, of moderate affluence, who has not his little gallery, which, with his music, his caleche and his pipe, form his favorite recreation from the fatigue of business'.[49] No Grand Tourist after 1815 got away from Frankfurt without visiting the statue of Ariadne sitting on a tiger, commissioned by Moritz von Bethmann from Dannecker of Stuttgart for 15,000 florins.

In France some bankers maintained their wealth despite the Revolution. An Englishman in Paris in 1801/2 found the home of the Parisian banker Jacques Récamier in the Chausée d'Autin furnished 'in a style of splendour exceeded only by the Tuileries'.[50] His wife was one of the luminaries of Parisian literary and political society during the Consulate. In Italy there was a division between nobility and commerce reminiscent of Frankfurt. The English socialite Mrs Hester Piozzi, attending mass in Milan in 1784, noticed a smart lady nearby, with two footmen. 'Who's that lady?' Mrs Piozzi asked her servant. 'That's no lady,' he replied, in a line worthy of music hall, 'that's a rich banker's wife.'[51] However, barriers in Italy were soon to break down. An American tourist in Florence noted that the banker Fenzi was well-established in the hierarchy of 'receiving'. What set him apart was not his own social position but his guest list which was 'subservient to business' – that is, it included guests from lower social orders whose money might one day be useful to him.[52]

In the company of such bankers the English Grand Tourist could generally feel quite comfortable; the social level was roughly what he himself was used to, and also what he associated with the status of the private banker at home. Should he wish, for whatever reason, to minimize these contacts, there were sometimes expatriate bankers to welcome his business, for instance in Paris, Rome, Moscow, and Galata, near Constantinople. There were also British merchants abroad who acted both as bankers and baggage handlers, like Ray at Montpellier, much praised by Smollett.[53]

Such merchants had long been the traveller's friend and shipping agent when the banking service in Britain was still restricted to the London goldsmiths. Even when reciprocal banking arrangements existed at international level, the role of the merchant, whether native or expatriate, was never wholly removed. This was because some countries, among them France, had no private bankers as such outside the very largest centres. A traveller from, say, Paris to Avignon would receive a bill of exchange from a Parisian banker drawn on an Avignon silk merchant. The tourist soon learnt that such a merchant was more properly known in French as a *négociant* (businessman) than a *marchand*.[54] The latter was often just a shopkeeper.

In more distant countries the practice of banking was sometimes difficult for the traveller to comprehend. Even in Turkey, only one step from Europe proper, the environment seemed a world apart. Local bankers were Armenians or Jews whose premises, among the public buildings of Constantinople, seemed second in consequence only to the mosques. Their wealth was achieved by a careful manipulation of the foreign exchange market whenever the Ottoman government prepared a new coin issue – a frequent occurrence on account of the debased national currency. Bankers drew bills on western Europe when the rate was high and then bought bills to balance their expenditure when the rate was low. The difference in value was instant profit.[55]

In another sense, however, banking in Turkey was attended by great risk. On the death of a public figure, or when someone was executed, the property of the deceased passed to the State. Men who perceived themselves in danger made over everything informally to their bankers. It was then a matter for the banker to disgorge such a sum, after the client's death, as would satisfy the State; if the figure was deemed inadequate he was tortured to produce rather more.[56] In Kashmir there were worse tribulations. The banker who helped George Forster of the East India Company to get a passport was desperate to avoid entanglement with the government, who had asked him for a loan. But refusal proved more injurious than impoverishment, as he was soon put to death.[57]

In the Far East the traveller found an illusive sense of familiarity. On the one hand there were branches of large joint stock companies, such as he knew in Britain from the mid-nineteenth century, like the Oriental Bank. But the method of accounting was bewildering. He stood in awe of the chaotic activity and desperation which accompanied the balancing of books before the Chinese new year. In Japan the barrister J.F. Campbell was bemused equally by the double accounting and the pidgin English – a language which George Train, an exasperated American tourist, had earlier characterized as 'that horrible jargon of mutilated baby-talk'.[58] Having presented his money order for payment, Campbell was sent with a note for a nominal sum of Mexican silver dollars (which were merchandise as well as money) to a cashier called a comprador, counting on a grid strung with beads. 'How muchee catchee?' asked the comprador. 'What you wantchee? No 1 dollar? Can do.' The comprador then, in effect, bought in the bank's own note and sold him Mexican dollars in exchange, leaving Campbell wondering why life was so complicated.[59]

In Australia, however, the mid-Victorian traveller felt more at ease. Banks *looked* like banks, at least in the big cities. There were no more white-washed rooms with a green cloth-covered table in the centre, as he had found in the Straits Settlements.[60] In George Street, Sydney, banks were 'choice specimens of architecture . . . great ornaments to the city'.[61] At Melbourne also, 'bankers have erected banking-houses on the Grecian model, with columns, porticoes, and the richest architectural facades',[62] while branch managers were assuming a high and respected position in the community. 'At the bank he is the stern man of business, but socially is a *bon vivant* [sic].'[63] Albeit at ten thousand miles' remove, the British traveller at last found a banking system with which he was entirely familiar.

But in moving so far afield, the story has anticipated the banking instrument which made such an excursion a credible proposition. It is time to return to Europe, and to the bill of exchange, and see how the traveller utilized the commercial relationships which worked so well without him.

2
COIN AND CREDIT: TOURISTS IN THE WORLD OF COMMERCE

Long before the guidebooks of Murray and Baedeker, the prospective traveller was never short of advice. The keeping of a diary, the learning of languages, the observation of society, antiquities and commerce, were all recommended to his attention. The most practical suggestions, including those as to money, were naturally from those who had been travellers themselves. William Wey was one of the first in the field: his guidebook for pilgrims to the Holy Land, published in the late fifteenth century, included a table of exchange rates.

There is a distinction between provision made beforehand for the supply of money abroad, and the money itself once the instrument of credit has been encashed. Of course, a traveller in the Middle Ages needed no credit arrangement at all if he had an entourage large enough to carry gold or silver bullion. In the early thirteenth century, for instance, the Bishop of Passau, on a journey to Rome, carried silver bars, each of the weight of one mark, which were exchanged as necessary against local currency. Similarly, unminted gold might be carried at any date, if the traveller was not too worried by his own security. An anonymous rambler from Sydney to Southampton claimed, even in 1847, that he paid 6 ounces of gold for his berth on a steamer from Peru to Panama.[1] But as most countries, from the Renaissance, prevented the removal of bullion and specie in any quantity from their own shores, so metallic money was always a disadvantaged form of provision.

An early victim of the English embargo on the export of money was Erasmus, who was allowed to take only 6 angels out of Dover in 1499; he therefore forfeited the balance of his money, amounting to some £20.[2] Travellers from Lyons to Italy in the sixteenth century were restricted to 80 crowns, and between Turin and Rome to 50. The French writer Babeau, looking back at this position from the nineteenth century, wondered whether such restrictions had not been engineered by bankers to support the bill of exchange.[3]

Fynes Moryson pointed out in 1617 that only £20 could then be taken out of England, a sum reckoned reasonable for the average journey. He mentioned the further restriction between France and Italy and warned against smuggling money as the Italian customs officers made vigorous searches 'never wincking at any delinquent'.[4] Moryson's feeling was that a large supply of specie was simply unnecessary given the alternatives which then existed, and in this he was backed up by James Howell, writing in 1642. Howell distanced himself from the earlier advice of Sir Thomas More, who 'wisheth one to carry always his Friends about him, abroad, by which hee means pieces of gold: Yet too great a number of such Friends, is an encomber and may betray him'.[5] When a money supply could be established by paper, a man who loads himself down with money, said Howell, 'is as wise as he, who carried the coach-wheele upon his back, when he might have trilled it before him all along'.[6]

A simple form of bill of exchange was the traveller's normal money order from the reign of Elizabeth. One copy was carried on the person, the other two sent ahead. Bills were obtained from London goldsmiths, or mercantile houses, against a deposit of money. Once the traveller was abroad he needed family or friends to maintain his credit, so that further bills could be despatched as necessary. Moryson recommended two bills a year, other writers four. The traveller also carried a covering letter (an 'advice'), which Moryson suggested should describe 'the most rare markes of your body', in case one of the thirds of exchange should be fraudulently presented before the traveller's arrival. He also recommended that the amount, weight and denomination of coin to be issued should be clearly specified.[7]

When banking in London became an independent profession, roughly from the Restoration, the role of mercantile houses in issuing tourists with bills diminished, unless of course the traveller had a family connection with such a house, as was quite often the case. For the convenience of a bill, the tourist paid a commission of around 10 per cent to his banker, but this figure could be as high as 15.[8] The banker also enjoyed the use of the money during usance, while the tourist paid further commission to the banker or merchant who encashed his bill. The drawbacks of using a commercial instrument were therefore quite high, but at least there was little risk of the bill being dishonoured. As international commerce was built on the bedrock of bills of exchange, the traveller benefited accordingly.

Dependence on England for a continuing supply of bills declined in the eighteenth century as it became possible to buy them locally, from town to town. English bills became useful only for the first leg of a journey (after the initial supply of ready money was exhausted); or as a means of sending money from father to son when the latter was on the Grand Tour under paternal scrutiny; or likewise from husband to wife when the latter, like Lady Mary Wortley Montagu at Venice, was domiciled abroad. An added advantage of the bill, when it was purchased locally, was that the traveller could avoid the money-changers. If the money in the country he was in could only be exchanged at a loss in the country where he was going, he could usually find a merchant or banker with an interest in both places who would give him a bill for the money he held, payable in the next country in appropriate specie. The commission paid on this deal could be lower than the loss by simple exchange of coin. This only worked, however, if there was a course of exchange between the two centres. A traveller in Dresden, for instance, could not get a bill on Hanover as there was no communication, in the technical sense, between them; he had to have a bill on Leipzig and another from Leipzig to Hanover.[9]

Letters of credit were suggested as a documentary alternative by both Moryson and Howell. Strict adherence to usance meant that some firms on whom bills of exchange were issued left the traveller waiting around until the maturity date. A letter of credit, on the other hand, was valid when presented, but the risks of fraudulent encashment were greater, and if the traveller lost his letter there were no duplicates, despatched under separate cover, to support it. Also, there was always the risk of a dishonoured letter as we have seen in Chapter One. Moryson implied that letters of credit might be encashed abroad without money being first deposited in England;[10] this might account for some of the rare refusals of payment, as the addressee might not know the solidity of the relationship between the tourist and his banker.

The real advantage of letters of credit over bills was in journeys between towns which had no course of exchange on each other. They were also used as an alternative to bills by travellers who required a flexible itinerary. Smollett, for instance, acquired letters of credit in Geneva in 1764 to pursue his journey to Florence and Rome,[11] and the Revd Mr Walsh used them between Constantinople and Bucharest in the 1820s.[12] Another point was that a bill of exchange, being drawn in a fixed sum, might prove too large or too small for the traveller's immediate requirement, loading him with unnecessary ready money, which might be dangerous, or forcing

A Russian post-house on the road from Kostroma to Jaroslav, about 200 miles north-east of Moscow. Only the most intrepid travellers ventured so far from the normal Grand Tour routes

him to re-negotiate with his supplier; whereas a letter of credit need not be paid to its full amount at the first presentation. Nevertheless, the bill of exchange and the letter of credit were very similar and some travellers' memoirs are inexact as to which they carried or received: Lady Mary Wortley Montagu can be forgiven for referring in 1740 to her 'bill of credit'.[13]

If the advantages of paper as against specie were obvious in Europe, they were less apparent in Asia where the climate was more hostile. George Forster, travelling through India towards Russia at the end of the eighteenth century, took bills of exchange from banker to banker in the larger towns on his route. There was no system for duplicates, however, and Forster had two dreadful experiences. The first one he just got away with:

On presenting my bill to the banker at Jumbo, I found, from its having been twice drenched in water, that the folds adhered together as firmly as if they had been pasted. The banker, with much good nature, soaking the paper in water, and opening the folds with care, was enabled to read, though with difficulty, the contents. Had he been disposed to protract the payment, there was sufficient cause; but holding out no demur, he at once said the bill was a good one, kindly observing also, that as my journey had been long and fatiguing, I should have brought an order for a larger sum.[14]

On the journey from Kashmir into Afghanistan his luck ran out. He had converted 500 rupees into a bill on Kabul which he kept tucked in a waistband. Becoming wet with sweat, the bill turned into a black smudge, almost illegible, which Forster hawked without success around all the local traders: 'not a merchant of the city, and all were applied to, would even attempt to decypher the paper, when he understood it contained an order for payment'. In the end, Forster sold it for half its nominal value to a Georgian with whom he was lodging. Thereafter he kept to specie.[15]

Despite the usefulness of paper credit in a kinder climate, the traveller still had the problems of metallic money to deal with once his paper was encashed. We have seen that banknotes were not uncommon in the age of the Grand Tour, especially in Scandinavia, but there were few countries in the more popular circuits where banknotes were welcomed with any consistency. This meant that long journeys by diligence, or river boat, or the hire of a *vetturino* (carriage), needed ready money. These sums could be considerable: it cost the equivalent of around £10 to go from Calais to Paris (usually the first point for encashment of a money order) and £30 from Paris to Lyons.[16] Shelley and his small party spent £60 in 1814 getting from Paris to Neuchâtel in Switzerland.[17] A nine-day cruise down the Lower Danube, from Pressburg to Galatz, cost 65 Hungarian florins (each 2s 1d), payable at embarkation – an awkward quantity to handle, even straight from the bank.[18]

Again, the traveller was not short of advice as to how metallic money should be carried and concealed. Fynes Moryson warned against showing large sums in wayside inns, where thieves had their informers. If asked where he was going, the traveller should give only a destination from town to town (as anyone announcing a long journey would be presumed to have money to match it). At night he should put his purse under his pillow 'always foulded with his garters, or some thing hee first useth in the morning' in case he forgot it. Moryson's last suggestion – prophetic of modern advice on mugging – was never resist an armed robber.[19]

With this advice, Moryson spoke from experience. In 1594, heading towards Paris from Metz, he ran into a troop of disbanded soldiers. He was carrying much more gold than he would have liked because the French civil wars had interrupted communication between Venice, his starting point, and Paris; so he had been unable to get a bill of exchange for any town past Geneva, where he took specie for the rest of the journey. Moryson let the soldiers search him and they stole his inner doublet, in which much of the gold had been quilted. But he had not lost everything. At Metz he had put 16 French crowns 'in the bottom of a wooden box, and covered them with a stinking ointment for scabs'. The soldiers tossed this aside. He had buried 6 other crowns in darning wool, stuck-through with needles, and the soldiers missed those as well.[20] On another occasion, travelling between Hamburg and Emden – a route infested with Spanish free-booters – he hid his gold in his shoes while trying to look as insignificant as possible; 'I bought an old Brunswicke thrummed hat, and made mee a poore Dutch suite, rubbing it in the dust to make it seeme old, so as my Taylor said, he took more paines to spoyle it, then to make it.'[21] The same trick worked a few years later for Thomas Coryate, hiking through Germany with gold quilted in his jerkin. He looked so decrepit, 'like a mendicant friar', that two potential robbers gave him money 'as paid for half my supper that night at Baden, even fourpence halfpenny'.[22]

In safer times, when money did not need quite such concealment, it was usual to wear some sort of body belt. One kind, still available in the mid-nineteenth century, was a buckled belt of chamois leather with a hundred buttoned pockets each capable of holding a gold coin the size of a sovereign. Such belts originated in the near East where the biblical word 'purses' in Matthew 10, verse 9 ('Provide neither gold, nor silver, nor brass in your purses.') would be more accurately translated from the Greek as 'girdles'. Travellers to Smyrna well into the nineteenth century picked up these belts or girdles in the bazaar: they passed once around the body and were then secured by a buckle. Successive folds obscured the fastening, while the end tucked in at the side of the waist.[23]

The particular problem in Turkey was the small, low-value money known as aspers. Moryson, who was in Constantinople in 1598, received 125 in exchange for a gold sequin, 100 for a French crown, and 75 for a German dollar. He found all business in the city was conducted in these little copper coins; in many deals they were impossible to count, so they passed by weight. In large contracts Moryson observed that 'they reckon by asses loads of aspers . . .'[24] Even with the later para (a coin worth five aspers in the nineteenth century, but still only one-eighth of a penny), there were problems. Made of impure silver, this money was said by one visitor to Smyrna to be:

as thin as a cobweb; the Turk counts them down, in little heaps of five at a time, on a board with a raised border, and sloping at the one end to a point, through which he pours them into his own bag, or the hand of his customer, whilst the rapidity, and at the same time the exactness, with which he spreads down a handful of fives, almost creates a smile at first sight; but never could we detect an error of a single one in his favour . . .[25]

The problem of small, low-quality coinage was not restricted by continent or date. As belts and purses swelled and strained, travellers from Sweden to Italy had dreadful visions of the death of Correggio, the early sixteenth-century Italian artist, who reputedly burst a blood vessel while trundling away a barrow-full of copper coin – his payment from the Duke of Modena for a painting. Some swore roundly, like H. Matthews in Portugal, with his 'travelling treasury . . . in a green baize bag', consisting of 150,000 rees, each worth about a quarter of a farthing;[26] others, like Captain Baldwin in Rome, drawing out £100 worth of Spanish dollars, simply found the pockets fell out of their trousers.[27]

The problem had not ceased by the time Mark Twain visited Tangier in 1867. His friend Jack tried to change a gold coin at a Jewish money-lender's and found he had broken the bank: 'eleven quarts' of coin were needed in exchange, forcing the man to negotiate on the street for the balance. Twain himself, never a man for understatement, claimed to have had 'nearly half a pint of their money' in exchange for a shilling.[28]

Travellers who carried most gold and silver about them, as opposed to the petty currencies, were those who went long journeys by sea. It was often impracticable to carry bills of exchange, as ships could be forced, by weather or other circumstance, into ports which they had not intended to visit. But if the isolation of ship-board appeared to diminish the risks of robbery, it was only an illusion. The menace of corsairs from the Barbary coast made any tourist on the Mediterranean Sea sweat with apprehension, even on a coastal voyage from Nice to Genoa, just as his forbears had done in the North Sea, when pirates sailed out of Dunkirk.

The most famous escape act from piracy was that of Queen Caroline who, when still Princess of Wales, began a long sea journey towards the Levant and the Holy Land in 1814. The expense of this considerable voyage, entailing appropriate hospitality at ports of call, was formidable, and the ship carried diamonds and specie to meet it. An unfortunate visit to Tunis put five pirate ships in hot pursuit, hounding the royal vessel from port to port. Three were caught by friendly governments but the

Mark Twain alleged that no new money was coined at Tangier, but that Jewish money-changers used vast quantities of low denomination coins four and five hundred years old – certainly one of his whimsical exaggerations, although 'hard' European currency was doubtless very welcome.

others came twice within sight in the drama of the chase. According to the narrative of the voyage, the princess was never too concerned, ingenuously believing that the pirates would rob them and leave, while her military advisers knew that capture would result in slavery for some, massacre for the rest, and the sinking of the ship.[29]

It is now time to consider one of the wider aspects of tourism – the way in which the traveller's foreign contacts were increasingly obliged to offer him more than a supply of money. To understand this properly, we have to realize that only the smallest continental excursion could be

Caroline of Brunswick-Wolfenbüttel (1768–1821), queen of George IV, a controversial and spirited lady, more popular with her subjects than with her husband. The journal of her Mediterranean voyages, written 'by one of her Majesty's suite', illustrates the very real dangers of a Grand Tour by sea before the menace of Barbary Coast piracy was brought under control

accomplished without the good offices of someone abroad. Clare Howard, who wrote a book on Renaissance travel in 1914, saw Elizabethan tourism as 'a very exciting form of sport, a sort of chase across Europe, in which the tourist was the fox, doubling and turning and diving into cover, while his friends in England laid three to one on his death'.[30] Although this simile is too dramatic for the following centuries, the Grand Tourist went from one bolt-hole to another gathering spiritual and worldly strength to complete his progress. The point of monetary succour was originally a mercantile house but became the local bank – or rather the local banker, in that the best society went more for the man than his place of business. It will be shown later under exactly what obligations the banker came to be placed, but first must be examined the wider issue of the 'letter of introduction', or 'recommendation', the instrument by whose rituals the merchant or banker was constrained.

Among the suggestions of Francis Bacon, in his essay on travel of the early seventeenth century, was that the traveller 'upon his removes from one place to another, procure recommendation to some person of quality residing in the place whither he removeth; that he may use his favour in those things he desireth to see or know'.[31] Similar advice, couched in the language of the day, was in every continental guidebook for the next two and a half centuries. Foreign writers were no less insistent of the advantage: '*Des lettres de recommandation*', wrote H. Langlois, '*non seulement*

Algiers, before colonization by the French in 1831. Once a notorious centre of organized piracy, it developed into a strong trading and financial centre, with several hundred bankers, brokers and money-changers, by the mid-nineteenth century

pour des banquiers solides, mais encore pour différentes personnes dans les autres conditions de la société, sont ou du moins peuvent être très-utiles. Ne dédaignez pas cette précaution.'[32]

Those who felt they could do without letters of introduction, in relatively more recent times, deluded themselves. A traveller of 1847, who had dismissed them in New South Wales as 'no better than waste paper', confessed to find them indispensable in a journey through South America: 'I would recommend all travellers to get as many as they can, never mind to whom.'[33] Without them he would have been rooked in hotels, mistrusted when cashing bank drafts, and excluded from local society. With them, he dined ashore with ships' agents on a voyage from Chile to Peru; found a muleteer to take him across the Panama isthmus; and had free sangaree (madeira and water half-and-half, plenty of white sugar, and two or three lumps of ice) in Kingston, Jamaica.[34]

The essence of the letter of introduction remained exactly as Bacon described it, while the definition of 'some person of quality' descended gradually through the levels of nobility and the diplomatic service and arrived ultimately at commerce and banking. From London to Paris, Denmark to Sweden, Constantinople to Bucharest, Benares to Cawnpore, the traveller kept his 'letters' next to his money orders and no less safely than his passport. Obviously, the more powerful the signatory, the better were the prospects of attention when a letter was presented. It is therefore refreshing to read occasionally of a much lower level of relationship: the traveller C.E. Dod presented a letter in Germany in 1820 'from the pen of a most invaluable personage – my washerwoman in London'. This woman had a daughter in service to a citizen of Hanau, married to an English lady, who were the addressees of the letter. The introduction worked perfectly and Dod was 'overloaded' with hospitality.[35]

If the obligations of addressees – who would usually have no knowledge of the traveller until he arrived at their doorstep – are considered more closely, a spectrum of responsibilities is revealed ranging from dinner and a bed, to a guided tour of the sights, to the payment of bills of exchange or the honouring of letters of credit. The monetary side was restricted to merchants and bankers, but in time they acquired the same duties of hospitality as had formerly belonged to the international Freemasonry of the aristocracy. An obvious reason for this extension of service was that bankers and merchants became increasingly landed and affluent, and occasionally titled.

We can therefore see the origins of travel services in mainland Europe as another aspect of *noblesse oblige*. Relations were often reciprocal: when Prince Pückler-Muskau of Germany called on the Earl of Essex in Hertfordshire in 1826, he was shown around by the earl's son-in-law whom he had already entertained in Dresden.[36] Such international fraternizing was oiled by the ability of the upper classes (among whom were many Grand Tourists) to speak at least one foreign language with reasonable fluency. Some English travellers, like Fynes Moryson, were exceptional linguists, coping even with Dutch; most spoke French quite well with often a working knowledge of German and Italian.

The best-educated travellers were amazed and delighted at the chance to speak Latin, which could act as a basis of mutual understanding even in Portugal, and certainly in eastern Europe. The Revd Mr Walsh was awoken one morning, in an obscure Hungarian inn, by the valet. '*Visne schnaps, Domine?*' asked the man, with a glass in his hand. '*Quid est schnaps?*' countered the clergyman immediately, whose Latin was better than his knowledge of alcoholic drinks.[37] Further east, in Turkey and the

Aleppo, now in Syria, anciently a very large and important trading centre on one of the overland routes to the East. The city declined in size and prosperity when a sea route to India was discovered via the Cape of Good Hope

Levant, Italian was spoken widely, as well as lingua franca – a mongrel language of French, Italian, Greek and Spanish origins. But French was the real commercial and diplomatic language of Europe, spoken in polite society in preference to the mother tongue, and given international acceptance for the text of passports and money orders. For the French traveller this was a delightful windfall. Fortia de Piles noted in his journal: '*l'universalité de la langue française (dans la bonne compagnie seulement) semble autoriser un Français a ne connoître que sa langue . . .*'[38]

Another level of service, offering a more practical relationship with the traveller, was provided by diplomatic staff. Ambassadors received the best visitors in chief cities but contact was more commonly with consuls, not necessarily of one's own country, who were at most regional centres of importance, especially the larger ports. Whatever their other duties, the extension of hospitality to travellers at government expense would appear to have monopolized their time. These men were held in universal high esteem, and not without reason, as a few instances will show. Fynes Moryson and his brother called on George Dorington, the English consul in Aleppo, in 1596, who 'most courteously entertained us, with plentifull diet, good lodging, and most friendly conversation, refusing to take any money for this our entertainment'.[39] Further into the journey, Moryson's

In contrast to the image of British consular officials, this sketch of the American consul to Tangier and his family depicts a scene of boredom and inactivity. In a European location, one suspects that tourists would have kept the consul much busier

brother died of dysentery, and he himself fell very ill. Dorington lent money on no security, which Moryson repaid on his return to England, 'yet I confesse, that I cannot sufficiently acknowledge his love to mee, and his noble consideration of poore and afflicted strangers'.[40]

The irascible Tobias Smollett, who could assassinate the character of an innkeeper or coachman with a few choice words, found the English consul at Nice, who lent him his lodgings, 'one of the best natured and most friendly men in the world'.[41] In the same town Arthur Young found in the consul 'both hospitality, and something too friendly to be called politeness'.[42] Visiting Denmark in 1774, the red-blooded Nathaniel Wraxall 'presented my letters of introduction to the English consul, Mr Fenwick, who received me very politely . . . Mr Fenwick's hock, and what was ten times more powerful, his lady's company and conversation . . .', delayed his itinerary.[43] As well as hospitality, consuls gave advice on passports, money, the state of the roads, and local politics. They also gave letters of introduction to the traveller's next destination, and were sometimes prepared to act as a *poste restante* for a suitably distinguished expatriate, like Lady Mary Wortley Montagu, living in Venice.[44]

Merchants and bankers were more often recipients of letters of introduction than the aristocracy or diplomatic staff. Such a letter took the place of the more businesslike 'advice' accompanying a bill of exchange, but if the traveller was carrying a letter of credit, then it became possible to dispense with any other written introductions, as 'a Letter of credit,' to quote one guidebook, 'is considered as a claim to the advice and friendly attentions of the Merchant or Banker to whom it is addressed'.[45]

Conversely, visits to such people abroad without letters of some kind, meant no socializing and sometimes a raw deal. Fortia de Piles, wandering in north Europe, met 'famous' bankers who, allegedly, gave him light-weight money for half of every withdrawal. '*D'après le défaut d'attention de personnes faites pour mériter la confiance,*' he mused, '*on peut juger de celle qui méritent les autres.*'[46] Testimonies to the fairness and good manners of bankers towards travellers who came unintroduced are by no means common, except perhaps in south Germany. A rare accolade in the annals of travel was given by Prince Pückler-Muskau to a rich Jewish banker in Rotterdam, where he called to collect sterling. The man 'behaved in the most respectful manner . . . It seems, therefore, that wealth has not yet made bankers so haughty here as at other places.'[47]

As has been shown, there was a closer affinity abroad between the professions of merchant and banker than English travellers were used to. This meant that for those who worried about such things, the social position of the merchant was problematical. Mrs Hester Piozzi, the socialite, found herself enchanted by the quality of her reception at Lyons. 'These are merchants, I am told, with whom I have been living,' she reported in surprise, her prose turning purple with enthusiasm: 'let the wealthy traders of every nation unite to pour the oil of commerce over the too agitated ocean of human life, and smooth down those asperities which obstruct fraternal concord.'[48] Similarly, Dr John Moore, the commentator on European society, had always felt that 'manners and conversations of merchants and manufacturers have been generally considered as peculiar to themselves'.[49] But in France, especially, he found them mature and cultured men; little difference existed between the *négociants* of Lyons and the courtiers of Versailles.[50]

Lyons was indeed the acme of mercantile hospitality, as well as a convenient centre for changing money, if one's host could be persuaded to put down his wine glass. Dr Rigby and his party had letters to Monsieur Rey, a *négociant* of Lyons, in 1789. They were taken to his country estate, 'picturesque beyond description', and introduced to his

The cathedral and bridge of Tilsitt at Lyons, showing also one of the picturesque wheel-cranes on the quays of the Saône. The prosperous and hospitable merchants of this thriving city, set at the confluence of the Saône and the Rhône, entertained many Grand Tourists on the main route from Paris to the Mediterranean

mother and three sisters, 'all very polite and one very handsome'. Rigby was astonished to learn that every merchant in the city had a country house like the one he was visiting.[51]

The Dutch family of van Tets, arriving in Lyons in 1819, were equally impressed. They had letters to the merchants Rast & Berger, and dined at the former's country house, which sounded similar to Monsieur Rey's. Then Madame Rast and her daughter guided the party through Lyons over two mornings, ending at the studio of the young painter du Clos, then very much in vogue. The next day Monsieur Berger took charge of the party and dined them at home. His daughter was about to be married and she and her mother regretted that 'the inconveniences inseparable from a wedding' prevented them extending the kind of welcome they would really have liked to offer. Then, Madame Rast took over again and accompanied her guests to a textile factory, her husband having given his word of honour that the visitors were '*ni fabricants, ni négociants, ni même Anglais*'.[52]

Dr Rigby's letters are something of a catalogue of mercantile hospitality, and show the full value of letters of introduction on a well-planned itinerary. He travelled from France into Italy, Switzerland and Germany, returning across Holland. At Marseilles, Monsieur Carthalan 'took us to several parts of the city', and at Turin Mr Negri 'accompanied us to many places'.[53] At Amsterdam the rich Mr Hope 'gave us tickets for the French play' and invited the party to his house and famous art gallery at Haarlem.[54] Arthur Young had reason to be grateful to a *négociant* at L'Orient in 1788, when he found all the inns full. 'I went directly to deliver my letters, found Mons. Besne, a merchant, at home; he received me with a frank civility better than a million of compliments; and the moment he understood my situation, offered me a bed in his house, which I accepted.'[55]

On the world stage there was no difference. Money-changing merchants protected Christians in Muslim Kandahar and secured admission for their guests to the Bengal Club in Calcutta, and to the billiard rooms and bowling alleys of Canton.[56] It is not easy to see *why* merchants remained so hospitable to travellers until well into the nineteenth century once their original reasons for association (baggage handling and money supply) were steadily usurped by shipping lines and bankers. Some merchants clearly valued their links with the issuers of bills of exchange or letters of credit, but it can hardly be argued that the mere potential of business outweighed such real entries on the debit side of the profit and loss book. It can only be concluded that merchants abroad, and particularly their families, enjoyed the social acceptability which the entertainment of foreign visitors entailed, and that they had reached such a level of cultural distinction themselves that it was a genuine pleasure to entertain the world's dilettanti.

Some of the groupings around merchants' dinner tables were truly cosmopolitan. Mr and Mrs van Tets, dining with a leading *négociant* at Bordeaux, found their fellow guests were a German lady, two Austrians, a Russian travelling with his wife, a Neapolitan, an Englishman, and a young Scotsman.[57] Only the last-mentioned, who had spent four years in Holland in the employ of Messrs Hope, was probably on business. This was by no means an urban phenomenon. In Transylvania the Revd Mr Walsh had letters to a Mr Popp, a Greek merchant in the small town of Hermanstadt. After dinner, a polite circle of twelve people assembled out of nowhere, including an Austrian princess and her father, a Greek baron, a Polish dissident nobleman, a Russian, a Saxon and a Wallachian.[58]

So rarely was the traveller let down by his reception that we feel as startled as he was at the disappointment. George Forster had an unfortunate experience in Asia where a merchant greeted him 'with a series of disgusting attentions', beginning by embracing his legs.[59] But that was a misunderstanding. Nathaniel Wraxall had a shock of another kind. He reached Memel in Prussia in 1774, hoping his letters to a mercantile house would give him a night on the town. 'I put on a suit of clothes which was more than decent: a pair of worked ruffles, and some powder thrown into my hair, made me, I thought, very smart. . . .' He then went jauntily to the merchants' address and became momentarily speechless. 'If the desks and bookcases . . . had not declared it to be a counting house, I should most certainly have mistaken it for a cock-loft. The casements were so completely covered with a crust of opaque matter, that no objects were distinctly visible through them. . . . Two black ill-looking figures . . . started up at the same moment, like Automatons actuated by springs . . . both dressed in deep mourning and weepers.'[60]

Wraxall sat on a stool, which had horse-hair escaping through the ruptured leather, and ventured mercantile small-talk. There was no enthusiasm on either side and the meeting soon petered out:

> I had now exhausted every topic of conversation: it was become so very dark, that I could hardly distinguish any parts of my companions, except their noses and their weepers: they had not given me an invitation, either to supper, or to dinner next day: the gloom increased every moment, while darkness and silence were drawing their mantle over us. – In a word, I found that I must go; so rising up, I made my bow, and wished them a good night.

He crept back to his lodgings 'half-mortified'.[61]

The fine divide between merchants and bankers must now be crossed to see what differences, if any, existed in the services of the latter. If hospitality is examined first, one forms the impression that fewer bankers than merchants made themselves socially available from the mid-eighteenth century, but that those who did entertained on a scale so lavish that some mark of superiority over merchants was consciously intended. Nowhere was this entertainment more prodigal than in Frankfurt. Charles Tennant had the honour to dine with Moritz von Bethmann in 1821, an experience which left him flattered, bewildered and defeated. When he arrived at the banker's summer residence he noticed a military guard of honour at the door, which suggested 'some princely visitor'. Sixteen guests eventually sat down to dinner in a dazzle of jewellery and decorated tunics. The company was congenial but the succession of courses 'continued until it became positively tedious', and he never did fathom the ritual of the wine:

Behind every three or four guests was stationed a man of majestic and warlike mien, clad in a richly ornamented uniform, with a cocked hat and high green feather. If, instead of standing behind my chair, he had been seated at the table, I, as a stranger, might reasonably have mistaken him at least for a field-marshal. A celebrated Saxon marshal, although apparelled in his military uniform, was certainly less imposing in figure and appearance. This noble-looking personage, however, behind the chair, was consigned to more ignoble duties, for his sole office seemed to be to help those submitted to his care to the proper wines after certain dishes.[62]

Hospitality aside, the remarkable aspect of the banker's contribution to the welfare of travellers, especially the Grand Tourist, was his role as a virtual travel agent. But that term is inadequate for the spirit of paternal concern which backed up assiduous attention to the traveller's worldly needs. The full extent of this role will be examined in the next chapter, once the concept has been introduced of the circular note, but bankers had been acting beyond the simple call of duty long before this innovation.

The letters of Lady Mary Wortley Montagu point to the earliest and most important of the continental banker's secondary roles – that of a *poste restante*. An inveterate correspondent, Lady Mary habitually complained of letters miscarrying or being opened by government agencies. Letters addressed to her via the bankers Belloni in Rome and Imbert at Lyons maintained the contact she needed with her husband in England, between 1740 and 1742. Belloni was particularly kind to her: we have already noticed that he gave her his last reserves of specie when the Roman economy was as flimsy as the paper money which supported it. As for letters, he had them delivered to her not only in Rome, but in Naples – an autonomous kingdom.[63]

A little later come the similar experiences of Smollett. 'I purposed to stay in Lyons', he wrote in 1763, 'until I should receive some letters I expected from London, to be forwarded by my banker at Paris.'[64] When he reached Rome, he found his banker there, Barazzi, acquired other uses. He asked him whether there was not a better way of returning to Florence. Yes, replied the banker, but unfortunately gave Smollett bad advice, and Barazzi joined the ranks of so many other Europeans, across the social spectrum, reduced to non-entity in a few wicked strokes of the Englishman's pen.[65]

It has now been shown how money and banking developed, and how the traveller, especially the Grand Tourist, adapted his monetary needs to the existing machinery of commerce. Also, the foreign banker has been spotted broadening the scope of his involvement with clients from foreign parts who came to him suitably introduced. In some areas the story has been

Lady Mary Wortley Montagu (1689–1762), depicted in Turkish dress. This redoubtable traveller and socialite went to Constantinople with her diplomat husband, returning to England in 1718 to introduce inoculation for smallpox. Later she settled in France and then Italy, notably Venice, whence she conducted a regular and (to our minds) very formal correspondence with her husband in England

taken well into the nineteenth century to follow a progression of ideas. Now it is time to revert to the late eighteenth century and look at a form of money order which was, eventually, to replace the bill of exchange, and in most cases the letter of credit, and give the traveller what he really wanted – an instrument tailor-made to his requirement. As in so many areas of banking, the innovator was a Scotsman. His name was Robert Herries.

3
HERRIES AND AFTER: THE 'CIRCULAR NOTE' AND ITS CONSEQUENCES

Today, the idea of closer links with Europe seems so topical and novel that we have lost any feeling of *déjà vu*. One of the great strengths, however, of British mercantile history has always been its continental and indeed international flavour. Chartered companies and merchant adventurers bridged cultural and political boundaries to an extent which disharmony between governments could scarcely interrupt. Entrepreneurs in finance and the commodities criss-crossed lines of international and colonial trade, developing enclaves of expatriate wealth.

One such enclave was of Scotsmen in Holland, where the mighty trading house of Hope & Co., centred on Amsterdam from the seventeenth century, produced a dynasty of merchants and bankers with unrivalled power and connections.[1] Rotterdam was equally favoured by the Scots and contained the mercantile houses of Crawford, Davidson, Herries, Livingston, and Manson. Our story begins with the house of Herries, maintained in Rotterdam by two brothers, Robert and Charles; the third brother, William, had a small estate at Halldykes in Dumfriesshire. When this William was in some financial difficulty in around 1750, he sent his son Robert to Rotterdam as an apprentice to his uncles. The young Robert discovered that one uncle, Charles, was dissolute, but the other, Robert, was a good businessman who was to play an important role in his nephew's aspirations.[2]

The real benefit to Robert in these early years, however, was the patronage he enjoyed from Hope & Co., who knew a promising young man when they saw one. Under their encouragement and protection, Robert Herries set up as a brandy merchant in Barcelona in 1754, aged twenty-three.[3] He took into partnership a Prussian, who had been his clerk in Rotterdam, and brought out from Scotland his two younger

Rotterdam, showing part of the harbour and the church of St Laurens. The city played an important role in the formative years of Robert Herries, innovator of the circular note

brothers, Charles and William. Soon he developed other business interests in Montpellier (Herries, Roy and Burnet) and Valencia, in the firm of Honorius Dadio & Co.[4] When Robert returned periodically to Britain it was with the stature of an experienced and respected merchant.

One particular Scottish friend from his Rotterdam days was John Coutts, partner in the Edinburgh house of Coutts Brothers & Co., corn dealers, commission agents, and negotiators in foreign exchange. The Coutts' connection with Rotterdam had been through their office there, managed jointly for many years with William Strachan.[5] One visit of Robert Herries to John Coutts at Edinburgh in 1761 was to set up a chain of events which altered the whole concept of travellers' money. At that time, of course, nobody envisaged what was just ahead. The first event was a double misfortune to the Coutts family which threatened to undermine their business interests.

For some years they had also run a London mercantile house, conducted by John's brothers, Patrick and Thomas; this was the correspondent of the Edinburgh house, handling the foreign exchange

Edinburgh, showing part of High Street, the commercial heart of the Old Town. The city was the birthplace of Coutts & Co. and was prominent in the careers of many other bankers, including Robert Herries and Sir William Forbes. It therefore has a special importance in the history of the circular note

side, and buying and selling goods on commission.[6] A fourth brother James (one of John's partners in Edinburgh) had left Scotland for the first time in his life, in 1754, to visit Patrick and Thomas in London. While there, he fell in love with, and married, the niece of George Campbell, then one of only two bankers practising west of Temple Bar. This union led to a partnership known as Campbell & Coutts which survived until 1760, when Campbell died. James then brought his brother Thomas into partnership to form a bank which is the direct forerunner of the present well-known business of Coutts & Co. Thus when Robert Herries arrived on the scene there were two distinct establishments of the Coutts family in London: the mercantile house in Jeffrey's Square, St Mary Axe, in the City, and the new bank in the Strand. Very much allied to the City house, but less closely to the bank, was the original Edinburgh concern, established in around 1723.[7]

The problems of 1761 arose when Patrick Coutts resigned from business on the grounds of ill-health, and later lost his reason; then, in August, John Coutts died suddenly in Bath. If the death of John was a serious blow to his fellow partners in Edinburgh, the loss of Patrick was nothing short of a disaster to the London house which the other partner, Thomas, had already left to join the bank in the Strand. New blood was urgently needed and Herries was too good a catch to miss. Terms were discussed and a new partnership created from Christmas Day 1762.[8] The fact that Herries was in a strong bargaining position is shown by the Coutts' agreement that he could continue to have an interest in his business in Barcelona. But he did not have his own way entirely, as we shall see.

The London mercantile house now became Herries, Cochrane & Co. under an agreement for twelve years with an option to break after three. William Cochrane was something of a liability, with no training or experience for the London markets. In fact he was a retired woollen draper, an uncle-in-law to the Coutts brothers who were simply concerned for his welfare.[9] Herries soon discovered that the imbalance between the partners in business ability was untenable and this was to be the first cause of tension between him and the Coutts family. The latter were becoming very successful and influential as bankers. They loaned money to the Jeffrey's Square concern at the outset of the new partnership and had insisted on the right to appoint a new recruit to the house in the event of a vacancy. 'To this privilege reserved to themselves by Messrs Coutts, Mr Herries strongly objected . . . [saying] that, as he would not allow any man to choose a wife for him, he had an equal dislike to a partner being chosen for him by anybody but himself.'[10]

This remark comes from the banker Sir William Forbes of Pitsligo. His memoirs, written in 1803 (three years before his death) were not published until 1860. Forbes was an intelligent and sensitive man who moved in the best circles of commerce and culture. He is the 'lamented Forbes' in one of the cantos of Sir Walter Scott's *Marmion* (addressed to Forbes's son-in-law), and the subject of a glowing tribute by James Boswell in his *Journal of a Tour to the Hebrides*. It was Boswell who had effected the introduction between Scott and Forbes, 'a man of whom too much good cannot be said . . .'.[11]

The particular relevance of Forbes is that he knew intimately all the

Sir William Forbes (1739–1806) of Pitsligo, friend and colleague of Robert Herries. Forbes was trained as a banker in the Edinburgh house of Messrs. Coutts and his *Memoirs*, published posthumously, are a vital source for the origins of the circular note

personalities in what became the Herries–Coutts altercation. His own private bank was to develop from the Edinburgh house of Coutts & Co., in which firm Forbes had served a long and rather austere apprenticeship.[12] Without his *Memoirs* little would be known of the dramas which underpinned the concept and implementation of the circular note, and nothing of the character of Robert Herries who has escaped notice in standard biographical sources.

Forbes received a one-eighth share in the Coutts' Edinburgh house in 1761, the year in which he first met Herries. He was therefore a signatory to the new agreements of Christmas Day in the following year. His *Memoirs* reveal him struggling with mixed loyalties to maintain a disinterested narrative. Letters and extracts are quoted which seek to convince that this agonized neutrality was maintained at the time. There is little difficulty in accepting this and in recognizing the dilemma of a man torn between a moral debt to the Coutts family for his own, albeit slow, advancement, and his instinctive admiration for the drive and foresight of Herries's inventive mind.

Herries had not long been in partnership in Jeffrey's Square before the situation moved from annoying to intolerable. It was simply that Mr and Mrs Cochrane, who lived on the premises, made no contribution to the profitability of the business. What was worse, Cochrane was in danger of doing real harm as an acting partner, as Forbes was forced to admit.[13] At the approach of the third year review point, Herries insisted that the Cochranes should go, while the Coutts brothers were adamant that they should not. To win the point, Herries had to dissolve the partnership. The Cochranes were bought off with life annuities to the lasting resentment of Messrs Coutts.[14]

In January 1766 the firm became Herries & Co. under a new contract to which Forbes and his two colleagues from the Edinburgh house (still known as John Coutts & Co., although with no Coutts representation) were signatories. James and Thomas Coutts, powerless to intervene from their banking house in the Strand, never overcame their grudge towards Herries, while Forbes and his Edinburgh colleagues were left in a limbo of embarrassment. 'I may safely say', wrote Forbes, 'that no incident of my life has ever given me half so much uneasiness'.[15]

In 1768 Forbes was in London nearly all the year 'as a guest with Mr Herries . . . attending the counting house'. In the evening they retired to Herries's fireside, and it was there, according to Forbes, that he first discussed his plan for supplying travellers on the Continent with a more useful system of credit. 'Mr Herries communicated to me not only the

John Coutts Esq.

LORD PROVOST of the CITY of EDINBURGH. 1742.

From a Painting by A. Ramsay.

John Coutts (1699–1751), the Edinburgh merchant and bill negotiator, from whose business the well-known London banking firm of Coutts & Co. was to develop

first idea, but every subsequent step of his plan till he brought it to a state of maturity.'[16]

Although, as has been seen, letters of credit were proving a more flexible alternative to bills of exchange, there were still disadvantages in their use, particularly if the traveller had no predetermined itinerary or was disposed to change his mind. To convince a foreign banker that he was worthy of letters to his next destination, the traveller needed ready money to buy his credit or an adequate expression of confidence from bankers in Britain. In the two or three weeks it took to arrange such confidence the traveller could again have changed his mind, or at best he was marking time.

Another considerable problem was the expense. At every stage of the renewal of letters of credit, travellers paid commission to local bankers. 'None of them', suggested Herries, 'take more than what is usual and just; yet, the whole added together . . . becomes a heavy tax on the traveller . . . according to the distance from the source. In a word, it is like buying goods of the second hand, or even of the third, fourth, fifth, &c. subject to the aggregate profit of all the different dealers.'[17]

The new plan, like most good ideas, was essentially simple: travellers could be issued with what Forbes explained as 'an universal letter of credit in the form of promissory-notes, which should be payable at all the principal places in Europe where travellers were likely to be'.[18] This called for a network of correspondents in main towns, who would be prepared to encash these notes at the current rate of exchange on London, without the charges or deductions which bedevilled the existing system. Instead, the correspondent banker would receive a commission from Herries, whose profit came from the use of the money laid out initially by the traveller in the purchase of the notes, until they came round again to London. Using the connection he had formed with Messrs Hope of Amsterdam, an adequate network of agents could easily be established.

The strong position of the Coutts brothers as West End bankers made it inevitable for Herries to offer them the opportunity to market the new scheme. Undoubtedly, he regretted this irony profoundly. In the wake of the Cochrane affair the two camps maintained a business connection but, in Forbes's words, 'there was no cordiality between them'.[19] The rebuff was predictable. Messrs Coutts replied that the plan 'did not suit them', and Herries had difficulty in selling his proposal elsewhere, despite praise for the merits of the concept.[20] In fact the scheme was so inherently sensible that the Coutts brothers could not afford to ignore it. The solution lay in a compromise: Herries would issue the notes through his

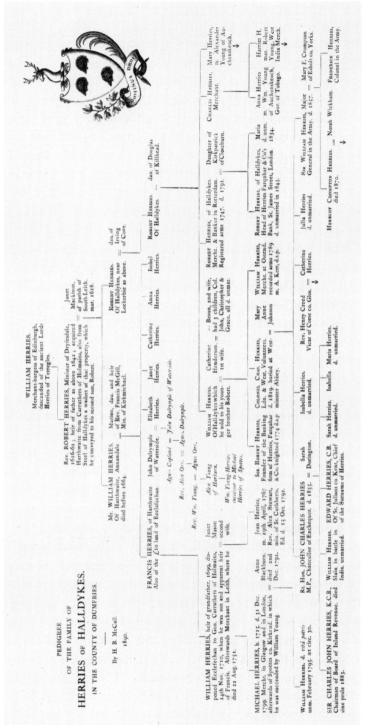

Sir Robert Herries and his pedigree. In the absence of a recorded portrait of the innovator of the circular note, he can at least be placed in the context of his family and forbears

own mercantile house and at his own business risk while Messrs Coutts would act as the retail outlet, drawing the attention of intending travellers to the new facility. This was probably in 1769, a year earlier than Forbes's tentative recollection.[21]

The arrangement did not last. Herries was soon complaining to Forbes that the Coutts brothers 'spoke of the plan . . . in so indifferent a manner to those who called on them for information, as rather discouraged inquirers from availing themselves of the notes than otherwise'.[22] He also believed they were attempting a scheme of their own, based in Paris. It was therefore a time for decisive action: Herries issued the new notes from his own mercantile house while proposing a new business venture to take over all aspects of the scheme. As principal partners he appears to have enlisted his uncle Robert, who had retired from business in Rotterdam, William Forbes (who had by then been knighted), and James Hunter (later Sir James Hunter Blair), who had been a fellow apprentice with Forbes in the Edinburgh house of Messrs Coutts.[23] As the law allowed up to six partners to operate a bank, which the firm technically was, two more recruits were needed, preferably to reinforce social credibility: these were William Pulteney (connected to the Earl of Bath and Lord Bradford) and Sir William Maxwell of Springkell, although neither was involved for long. The new venture was known as the London Exchange Banking Company, with an office at 16 St James's Street. There are, however, doubts as to the exact composition of the early partnership, and also its date of establishment. Forbes states categorically 1 January 1772, although he must be wrong: surviving papers (mostly in French, as the commercial language of Europe) begin nearly three years earlier.[24]

The London Exchange Banking Company offered quite a range of financial services for the British traveller in Europe. The main document for sale was initially called an 'exchange note' (*billet de change*), a name soon changed to 'circular note' (*billet circulaire*), although in some nineteenth-century literature the earlier name was occasionally revived. Such notes were issued with a circular 'letter of order' listing the towns where they could be encashed and acting as an introduction to the foreign banker. By 1770 correspondents had been found from Gibraltar to Moscow and from Stockholm to Prague. Circular notes were available in denominations no lower than £20 after the French Wars, but the earliest issues of the 'Plan', or prospectus, mention no minimum figure.[25]

Nominally, circular notes were payable seven days after sight, but this was simply to give the correspondent banker some breathing space if he

P L A N of Exchange Notes.
For the use of British — Travellers &c. in Foreign Parts.

1.° These Notes are signed by Mess. Herries & C.° in virtue of a power of attorney from the London Exchange-Banking Company, composed of six Members, jointly responsible for the value.

2.° Noblemen, Gentlemen &c. on their going abroad, or their Bankers & Agents, from time to time, during their absence, may invest any Sum in Exchange Notes, that their occasions require; And also have that Sum divided into as many Notes, as may best suit their convenience.

3.° The Circular Notes are made payable to order, but for mutual safety, must only be endors'd to the Agents abroad, by way of receipt for the amount in foreign Specie, on giving at the same time a duplicate of that receipt to serve in justification of the said Agents, towards the Company.

4.° They are engraved in French and entitled Billets de Change, with a general address, referring to the Agents of the Company, at the various places mentioned in an Alphabetical List, subjoind to the Circular Letter of order, given along with them, to each Traveller.

5.° The time of payment will be seven days after presentation (without any days of Grace) this short term being thought safer for the possessors, as well as the Agents, than orders at Sight, since, in case if any Notes being lost, there will be time to give Notice at the adjacent places, in order that the payment may be stop'd, and the value recover'd of the Company, on giving such Security as is usual on the like occasions.

6.° If however the Traveller should, to answer any particular purpose, have occasion for immediate payment, it will not be refused, on his satisfying the Agent, which he may easily do, of his being the Identical Person.

7.° None of the usual charges to which Travellers are subject, on receiving their Money abroad by means of Letters of Credit will be deducted on paying of these Notes; since the Company allow their Agents a sufficient Commission. Thus the Traveller will receive the full value, reduced into foreign Money at the current usance course of Exchange on London at the time of payment: Or, if there be no direct Course, by taking the medium of some third Place, as Exchanges vary almost every Post, he will sometimes receive more, sometimes less, according to these variations.

8.° As the Circular Notes, cannot be endorsed, or given in payment abroad to indifferent Persons indiscriminately. The Company, in order to adapt a Branch of this Plan to a more general use, will also issue Exchange Notes Transferable by simple endorsement, but payable by their Agents at some certain Capital Place, and for any required sums, previously reduced into the money of that place, or Country, at the last quoted Exchange from thence on London. Thus these Transferable Notes, equally free of every charge at payment, will answer in foreign Parts all the purposes of Bank Post Bills in England.

9.° The Company will take Bills of Exchange, of Drawers or Endorsers of undoubted Credit, on most of the Places contain'd in their list (even tho there be no Exchange at London on such Places) on such terms as may probably prove a means to save to the Possessors, the Commission and loss of time, in sending them for negotiation, to third Places on the Continent.

10.° Altho the use of Letters of Credit cannot be recommended to Travellers, yet to such as may require them for particular purposes, the Company will, on being satisfied of the Security, give circular or direct Letters of Credit, on Places which have a regular Exchange on London, subject only to the single Commission of their Agents, and postage at the Place of Payment; and another to the Company, which will both be exacted openly, and the money paid abroad, at the just course on London.

Lodgements for Exchange Notes will be received at
The Company's Office in S.t James's — Street, London
or by
Mess.rs Herries & C.° Jeffries — Square S.t Mary Axe — and

on leaving at either of those Places a memorandum of the Names &c. the Notes, together with the corresponding Letters of order, will be immediately prepared & sent, as directed, to any part of the Town. Any person desirous to know the Security, may at the same places be particularly informed.

'Plan of Exchange Notes', *c.* 1770. The word plan was used in those days to denote something more akin to a prospectus in modern terms. In this document – probably the earliest statement of what he was trying to achieve – Herries also introduced the concept of transferable notes, which differed from circular notes in so far as they could be endorsed abroad and given to a third party. The general term exchange notes was used to summarize the various kinds of paper which Herries was proposing

had reason to suspect a fraudulent presentation. Herries always made it clear that payment should normally be immediate. Sterling was to be converted into local money at the current usance course of exchange on London; or if there was no direct course, by taking the medium of a nearby centre which had such a course, among which Amsterdam, Paris, Madrid and Genoa were recommended.[26] No deductions were permissible by the paying bank except when certain kinds of coin could only be issued at a premium (or 'agio'), a matter out of the banker's hands. The traveller signed two receipts: one was the back of his circular note, which the agent sent back to Herries in London, who reimbursed it, adding a payment for commission of 1 per cent; the other was kept by the agent.[27] Accounts were settled every six months. From the traveller's point of view, the circular note abroad was wonderfully akin to what we now call a traveller's cheque.

Secondly, there were so-called transferable notes. These could be passed around by endorsement, but were payable (without deduction) only at one predetermined place. Herries envisaged them as useful for remitting money to people permanently resident abroad.[28] Thirdly, were circular letters of credit given for fixed sums, which could be drawn in whole or in part on presentation of a letter of order. But these were subject to payments for commission and postage to the agency bank and also to a further commission in London if Herries had not previously received value (i.e. the money or adequate security) for the amount. Herries was clearly out to supersede letters of credit as the tourist's main type of money order and always stressed that he could not recommend them.[29] They were so popular, however, with classes of society not too bothered by accumulated charges that he could not afford to omit them from his portfolio. Direct letters of credit, the fourth type of document on offer, were only different in that they were addressed to one place.

The tourist and traveller now had a total European monetary service, a market which Herries estimated as worth £1½ million a year.[30] Soon, letters of order gave the names of Herries's agents within any given town – a very desirable advance, as most large towns had several banks. For the London Exchange Banking Company the commercial risk attaching to circular notes was minimal as the partners already had their clients' money before they set out. Obviously, the risks to foreign bankers were more real, and they had to wait a long time for their profit margin. How Herries succeeded in setting up seventy-eight European agencies by 1770 speaks eloquently of his determination and influence, as well as of the support of Messrs Hope of Amsterdam. Not for nothing do they appear first in the lists of correspondents, in an otherwise alphabetical sequence. Soon the number of agencies rose to ninety-one, but within roughly the same boundaries. Constantinople and two locations outside Europe – Smyrna and Aleppo – were established by 1790 when the list of agencies totalled 141.[31]

It was essential for the success of the plan to persuade agents to pay out immediately in all normal circumstances, regardless of the seven days'

Lettre d'ordre

Londres ce 9 Sept.r — 1775

Messieurs

Madame la Comtesse Nous remettons cette lettre circulaire à M. de Salis née Fane pour la garder auprès d'elle et lui servir de guide au payement de nos Billets de Change circulaires. Nous vous prions de faire l'honneur requis (sur un double acquit) à ceux qu'il pourra vous présenter aux places respectives de votre résidence. Vous en reconnoitrez l'authenticité aux indices sousentendus. Nous prenons la liberté de recommander le dit dam. à vos politesses, et avons l'honneur d'être très parfaitement

Messieurs

Dans divers endroits les espèces en Or sont rares et content quelque prime, qui doit rester à la charge des Voyageurs, ou se compenser dans le change, puisque notre plan ne les excepte que des frais ordinaires. On remarquera aussi que les correspondans dans l'Etranger ainsi que les Raisons de leurs maisons, sont sujets à des changements.

Vos très humbles et très obéissans Serviteurs

Pour la Compagnie de Banque en Changes de Londres.

Robert Herries &c.

Amsterdam	M.rs Hope & C.o
Aix la Chapelle	J. M. Schmits & C.o
Aix en Provence	Beraye & Grepire
Alicante	Wombwells & Arabet
Angers	Parage
Anvers	Théodore Van Moorsel
Augsbourg	J. & G. G. de Halder
Avignon	Seste
Barcelone	Robert Herries & C.o
Barège	les voyageurs qui prennent les eaux à ces endroits se pourroient d'argent
Bagneres	à leur passage par Toulouse, Bordeaux, ou Bayonne
Bayonne	Dom.e Cabarrus l'ainé
Berlin	les Héritiers de feu David Splitgerber.
Berne	

T. S. V. P.

Herries gave a list of his correspondents on each letter of order. The first page of one such letter, dated 1775, is reproduced above. The style of the opening paragraph changed little over the next fifty years or so, although the document itself was later called a letter of indication. It served to introduce the customer to the foreign banker and contained a specimen signature. Also, Herries took the opportunity to warn his customer that if notes were encashed for gold coin, there would be a premium – something the plans had not indicated.

Particularly interesting in this document is the inclusion of Barège and Bagnères, two French watering-places close to the Pyrenees. Each was too small to have a banking-house, but Herries's customers wished to go there and provision had to be made for them. The two towns were later excluded from the agency list, but reinstated after the French Wars

COVER

For Notes, Letters of Credit, &c. in the Courſe of the Banking Buſineſs of Sir ROBERT HERRIES and Co. of London, with a fuller Liſt of the *Continental* Places of Payment than could be contained in their *General Letter* of *Order*, in which however any of the additional names will be occaſionally interlined.

Abbeville	*Breſlaw*	*Gibraltar*	*Middelburg*	*Rotterdam*
Aire in Artois	*Bruges*	*Gottenburg*	*Milan*	*Rouen*
Aix la Chapelle	*Brunſwick*	*Gottingen*	*Modena*	*San Lucar*
Aix in Provence	*Bruſſels*	*Hague*	*Montbelliard*	*Schaffhauſen*
Aleppo	*Cadiz*	*Hamburg*	*Montpellier*	*Smyrna*
Alicant	*Caen*	*Hanover*	*Moſcow*	*Spa*
Altena	*Calais*	*Havre de Grace*	*Munich*	*St. Maloes*
Amiens	*Carthagena*	*Heſſe Caſſell*	*Nancy*	*St. Omer*
Amſterdam	*Chamberry*	*Inſpruch*	*Nantes*	*St. Peterſburg*
Ancona	*Cherſon*	*Koningsberg*	*Naples*	*St. Quentin*
Angers	*Coblentz*	*Lauſanne*	*Narva*	*Stettin*
Anſpach	*Colmar in Alſace*	*Leipzick*	*Neufchatel*	*Stockholm*
Antwerp	*Cologne*	*Liege*	*Nice*	*Stolpe*
Augsbourg	*Conſtantinople*	*Liſbon*	*Niſmes*	*Stoutgard*
Avignon	*Copenhagen*	*Liſle*	*Oporto*	*Straſburg*
Barcelona	*Dantzick*	*Leghorn*	*Orleans*	*Tain*
Basle	*Dieppe*	*L'Orient*	*Oſtend*	*Tarbes*
Bayonne	*Dijon*	*Lubec*	*Padua*	*Toulouſe*
Berlin	*Douay*	*Lyons*	*Paris*	*Tours*
Berne	*Dreſden*	*Madrid*	*Parma*	*Turin*
Beſançon	*Dunkirk*	*Magdeburg*	*Perpignan*	*Valencia*
Beziers	*Duſſeldorff*	*Malaga*	*Pons in Saintonge*	*Valenciennes*
Bilboa	*Elſineur*	*Manheim*	*Prague*	*Venice*
Blois	*Florence*	*Marſeilles*	*Ratiſbon*	*Verona*
Bologna	*Franckfort on the Mayne*	*Maeſtricht*	*Rheims*	*Vienna*
Bordeaux	*Geneva*	*Mentz*	*Riga*	*Warſaw*
Boulogne ſur Mer	*Genoa*	*Memel*	*Rochelle*	*Yverdun*
Bremen	*Ghent*	*Metz*	*Rome*	*Zurich*

This Buſineſs is now ſo generally known as not to require any other explanation than is contained in the Notes, &c. themſelves; and thoſe of the *Branch* at *Paris* (carried on in the Name of *Sir Robert Herries* alone) anſwer every purpoſe of ſaving and utility to the Travellers who take their departure from the Continent, that the others of the Houſe in London do, to thoſe going from Great Britain and Ireland.

Both Deſcriptions of Travellers may alſo, without riſk, have new Supplies from Time to Time by Poſt, as the *circular* as well as *transferable* Notes are payable to Order, and none given, to the *Bearer*, but when required for particular or private Purpoſes.

Tourists received their notes in a 'Cover', like this one of *c*. 1790, which updated the information in the letter of order. Many of the 140 places named here are unfamiliar to us in the way they are presented; Havre de Grace, for example, is now known as Le Havre and Ratisbon is Regensburg

grace to which they were legally entitled. Herries was concerned for travellers '*d'un certain Rang ou Credit*', as he put it,[32] who could be influential in the areas they were visiting; a bad experience could lead to unfortunate publicity for circular notes and the need to change an agency. A greater act of persuasion was needed to wean agents from their taste for multiple commissions, and it was necessary to offset these by indicating some compensatory gains. These could be found, Herries suggested, by savings in the realm of entertainment. '*Nous n'entendons donc pas*', he wrote to correspondents, '*que vous deviez faire des fêtes à nos recommendés, ni perdre votre tems [sic] pour les courtiser. Ils se contenteront bien de vos expressions obligeantes et attentions ordinaires.*'[33] In this, however, he was to be proved wrong, as we shall see later.

Ironically, the main problems for Herries were not in Europe but in England. He had some success advertising his scheme directly to the nobility and upper classes, both by sending out 'cards' and by recommendation, but the support of London bankers was urgently needed. He had been prepared for 'the natural prejudice of mankind against every new thing' but the resentment of other bankers towards the London Exchange Banking Company seemed unwarranted.[34] In the printed *Remarks on the Plan*, Herries could see no reason why the Bank of England, or London bankers, especially those with a mainly domestic market, should suppose his scheme to interfere with their own business.[35]

The fact was, of course, that many of them felt his ideas would not end there, and envisaged the possibility of a secondary and wider banking practice, seducing their best customers by the initial enticement of circular notes. The same point was worrying Forbes. Already upset by the strained relationship between Herries and the brothers Coutts, he felt any attempt to attract regular banking business would make matters considerably worse. He therefore asked Herries what his intentions were. 'This produced an answer from Mr Herries, avowing that he had no intention to decline any banking business which might accompany the transacting of the travellers' notes, and then it was that I became fully sensible of the real nature of the plan.'[36] Forbes was in an agony of divided loyalty: Herries was his friend and he was a partner in the new enterprise, but he was also a partner, with Herries and Hunter, in the Edinburgh house (still known as John Coutts & Co.) whose main business was with Messrs Coutts in London.

In January 1772 Herries and Forbes entered into a strained correspondence on the ethics of poaching business. Herries felt that he had received such little support from the banking fraternity that he owed nothing in return:

We thought at first that Messrs Coutts and the other bankers in general would have favoured our plan, while we steered clear of any connection in their business. But the reverse has been the case with them all; and we believe none of them have applied for our notes, but when expressly ordered by their customers so to do, and in this way we have issued more in proportion to indifferent banking-houses than to those appointed to receive our lodgments. . . .[37]

What was really happening, Herries suspected, was that other bankers were planning the business of circular notes for themselves. But as agency networks took time to organize, Herries could count on two or three years without any serious rival. In that time he needed to build up a regular banking business to offset any fall in profitability from the competition which lay ahead. The wisdom of this ancillary activity was to be tested seriously by the French Wars and the virtual closure of Europe to Grand Tourists.

During this period Herries did not neglect his mercantile house (Herries & Co.) which had moved to Oxford Court in Cannon Street in around 1769. To strengthen his standing across the Channel, he won the commission from the Farmers-general of France to purchase tobacco on their behalf in Glasgow, the place of import. This deal with the French came to grief in 1775 (a year after Herries was knighted) for reasons which do not concern us, but Forbes felt that Herries was not blameless for the loss.[38] Relationships again became strained and the end of the London Exchange Banking Company followed quickly. It was, in any case, high time that the anomalous and convoluted connections between Herries, Forbes, Hunter and the Coutts brothers were resolved. Herries resigned from the Edinburgh house, while Forbes and Hunter resigned from both Herries & Co. in Cannon Street and from the Exchange Bank in St James's Street.[39]

The latter then became Sir Robert Herries & Co., a private bank with a speciality in travellers' money, while the mercantile house appears to have ceased trading altogether. Forbes, always the peacemaker, claimed that his break with Herries was not without cordiality; but this is rather difficult to believe, as the manner of the severance caused embarrassment to Robert Herries, the uncle, the other founding partner in the Exchange Bank.[40] The vacancies caused by the departure of Forbes and Hunter were filled by Charles and William Herries, the brothers whom Robert had first taken into business with him at Barcelona some twenty years earlier. The other partners (to complete the six allowed by law) were Thomas

Tho.ᵃ Hammersley Esq.ʳ

Drawn & Engraved by M. N. Bate.

Thomas Hammersley is one of the pivotal figures in the early history of the circular note. His career began with Robert Herries, but in 1795 he established with others a new bank at 76 Pall Mall. Hammersley became one of the major providers of tourists' money and the sudden failure of his banking-house in 1840 caused consternation among many of his customers. Following the crash, Coutts & Co. stepped in to rescue most of the business

Hammersley, who will reappear below, and Charles Sackville. The latter, never prominent in the bank, died in Venice in 1795.[41]

To what extent Herries's initiative was copied by others before the French Revolution is uncertain. That others did copy some of his proposals is clear from the 'Short Observations' which Herries issued to update his agents on minor extensions to the service 'beyond what has as yet been imitated'.[42] Unfortunately for Herries, his main competitor proved to be Thomas Hammersley, fostered in the bosom of his own firm. It would be interesting to know more about Hammersley's background and by whose influence he had succeeded to a partnership in the London Exchange Banking Company in around 1773. By the late eighteenth century West End banking was flourishing through a nexus of kinship, patronage and mutual convenience. The Hammersleys were connected with the Greenwoods, who were cousins of Richard Cox, banker and army agent in Whitehall. Cox himself had had a brief partnership with Henry Drummond, and took a paternal interest in Thomas Hammersley's welfare. Perhaps it was Cox who introduced Hammersley to Herries or Forbes; certainly it was Cox who stood surety for Hammersley when he left Herries in 1782 to join a new partnership with Ransom & Morland at 57 Pall Mall.[43]

This new firm was a bank first, and a provider of travel money second, but it was due to Hammersley as much as to Herries that the concept of the circular note sailed out of the doldrums of the Herries–Coutts disagreement to become the main money order of the continental tourist. Much of Hammersley's success followed from his winning the account of the prodigal Prince of Wales (later George IV) in 1787, which raised his banking service to an enviable level of influence.[44] In 1795 Hammersley left the partnership to form his own banking firm at 76 Pall Mall. (This business later came to grief, in 1840, stranding many travellers abroad without provision.) Thus by the end of the eighteenth century there were three issuers of circular notes in St James's with scarcely three hundred yards between them.

The firm, however, which Herries most feared was Messrs Coutts. It was no doubt with their competitive potential in mind that he formed a Paris branch in 1786 in the offices of Girardot Haller & Company.[45] Here, and at Herries's Paris residence opposite the Pont Royal, circular notes payable in French money at the usance course of exchange on Paris, were issued solely in the name of Sir Robert Herries. Herries himself spent two-thirds of the year in London during which time his Paris affairs were handled first by one John Forbes, and then by James Carey.[46] By 1788 his

Paris, showing the Pont Royal in the foreground, near to which Robert Herries issued 'Circular Notes' from his local residence. Many buildings in this view were destroyed by fire in the disorders of 1871

French colleagues had ceded to him the whole office, but the timing could hardly have been worse. Although the Revolution of 1789 was not itself an insuperable blow to the tourist trade, the acute shortage of ready money, linked to the issue of assignats, forced Herries to introduce for the French market a special kind of circular note, payable for relatively small sums between 24 and 192 livres tournois (i.e. 1 to 8 guineas at the pre-Revolution rate of exchange).[47]

This was in May 1790. At the same time he thought it wise to issue a printed statement confirming, as he hoped, his credibility with the French populace. He reminded them that for several years he had handled the commission in Britain for the purchase of tobacco for the Farmers-general, and that his current intentions were not in any way to encroach on the rights of anyone else, and still less on those '*du Public*'.[48] His experience in England had taught him that the banking system could work to the good of the general public, and vice versa.

By October he realized he would be better off in England. He wrote to all his correspondents referring to 'these critical times' and hoping 'to have no occasion after returning to England . . . to go across the channel any more'.[49] He was a tired and frustrated man. Carey, who was also in business on his own account, stayed on to manage the Paris branch,

stressing to customers that it enjoyed British protection and was therefore
to some extent immune from the chaos around it: in particular, its funds
were invested in foreign bills of exchange rather than French assignats.[50]
In 1795, or soon after, Carey surrendered the agency to A.J. Pochet,
presumably a Frenchman, and its affairs were not liquidated until early in
1797.[51] As England had been at war with France since February 1793, it is
amazing that the branch continued for so long.

Although his business affairs were well enough diversified to offset the loss
of travel income, Herries's aspirations were ended by the French Wars. With
his two brothers, he had kept alive the commission house in Barcelona, but
brought in new blood in 1792.[52] It had also been time to restructure the
bank in St James's Street. With no children of his own, Herries had
persuaded his cousin, also called Robert (son of Robert, partner and uncle)
to join the firm; he proved most capable. Robert the uncle died in 1791.
Herries himself felt it time to retire when the Paris branch was abandoned.
Sick and disillusioned, he wrote his last letter to customers on 17 March
1798, confirming his resignation in favour of two managing partners: his
cousin, and a relative newcomer, Thomas Harvie Farquhar.[53] The name of
the firm henceforth was Herries, Farquhar and Company.

It is impossible not to feel sympathy for Herries. Baulked by other
bankers, double-dealt to some extent by the French over the tobacco
commission, his thunder stolen by Hammersley, he was finally beaten by a
war which ended his vision of '*un genre de Banque circulaire*' conceived in
the heady year of 1788.[54] Centred in London and Paris, and unifying the
out-stations of European and Mediterranean travel, the bank could only,
he thought, become increasingly useful and robust '*puisque les risques sont
toujours diminués par la division, tandis que l'objet se multiplie pour ceux qui y
succéderont après moi*'.[55] There is no doubt that he was an egocentric and
single-minded man, ambitious to a fault, but he deserves better from the
history of travel than the niche of neglect assigned to him.[56]

There is evidence to show that, even with Britain and France at war,
the movement of travellers through France did not entirely cease. Letters
and specimen plans were still being sent to correspondents in France until
1795, with the list of agencies now extended to Algiers, Malta and
Cyprus.[57] However, the disruption of postal services meant that many
circular notes went astray. There was nothing new about lost notes; it was
the scale of the problem which was different. Sometimes it was not a
postal problem at all; the traveller simply lost his notes or had them stolen.
No great harm was done as long as he had not also lost his letter of order.
If he had, then his signature could be forged and the notes fraudulently

1794

Lettre d'Ordre générale

adressée aux Correspondans dans les

principales villes sur le Continent

de L'Europe

pour le paiement des Billets Circulaires

de Sir Robert Herries & Cⁱᵉ

de Londres.

Addenda

Villes		Correspondans
Angers	MM	Goslin de la Renrerie
Civita Vecchia	—	Alexⁱ Sloane
Dresde	—	Albⁱ Fredk Gregory
Francfort	—	Freres Bethmann
Geneve	—	Nadal & Robin
Lille	—	P. Questroy
Milan	—	Freres Rougier
Padua	—	Laurⁱ Onesti
Tain	—	Sourdan
Tournay	—	Piat Lefebvre & fils
Treves	—	Antⁱ J. Recking
Trieste	—	Phil. Griot
Vicenza	—	Freres Calvi
Naples	—	Macaulay Mackinnon & Cⁱᵉ

As the French Wars began seriously to impede the Grand Tour, the business of acquiring new agencies was, frustratingly for Herries, reaching full momentum. These extra bankers were added in manuscript to the newly printed letter of order of February 1794

presented. In today's terms, it is the problem of having one's cheque card stolen with the cheque book. Herries took great pains to warn his customers to keep the two elements apart, and his annoyance with General Hyde, who lost £200 worth of circular notes issued in 1789 together with his letter of order, was not concealed in a letter to correspondents.[58] By 1793 Herries was issuing agents with very much the kind of 'Cashiers' Warning' circulated today between clearing banks. Notes also got lost on their return journey from the agencies, after encashment, and it is not clear what provisions were introduced to allow for this, nor what happened about replacement notes for the careless or unfortunate tourist.

It is useful to digress here and consider theft in more detail. The high level of adult illiteracy in the late eighteenth and early nineteenth centuries meant that the loss of any form of money order was a less worrying problem than it is today. In Henry Fielding's novel *Tom Jones. The Adventures of a Foundling*, first published in 1749, the beggar who finds a bill of exchange for £100 in Sophia Western's pocket-book has an instinctive feeling for its value but curses the lack of a charity school education for his inability to read it. There is little record in the annals of travel of money orders of any kind being fraudulently presented, and it must be significant that Herries's circulars always referred to notes as '*perdus ou égarés*' (lost or gone astray) rather than stolen.[59]

Against this background, the experience of Sir George Lefevre, who travelled through France in 1843 as personal physician to a nobleman, becomes quite interesting. At Tours he was asked to encash one of his patron's circular notes, issued by Messrs Hammersley, for £100. Lefevre crossed the Loire bridge and arrived at the banking house where he found, to his disbelief, that he had lost it. 'I retraced my steps, trembling with agitation as I passed along, looking into every hole and corner of the street.' When he was back on the bridge, a little boy ran up saying his mother would like to speak to him. Lefevre could hardly take it all in: 'her lad had seen another lad, whose mother had seen a walnut woman, whose lad had picked up a piece of paper in some part of the town, and given it to his mother, who had taken it home, not knowing what it was'. Lengthy enquiry led to a distant part of the town where women were cracking walnuts. One of these women led him back to the banker's house where the missing paper had been surrendered in the meanwhile. When Lefevre had recovered his composure he spent some time wondering whether this was honesty or ignorance. In any event, the walnut woman was more satisfied with her reward than was Tom Jones's beggar man.[60]

NOTE de Billets Circulaires de *Sir Robert Herries & Co.* de Londres *perdus* ou *egarés*, & dont leurs Correspondants sont priés de refuser le payement en cas de presentation.

No.	£.		
1808 - - - - - - - - -	25 -	ordre *Joseph Webb* - - - - -	daté le 27 Novembre 1781
3414 - - - - - -	20 -	—— *John Boys* - - - - - -	—— 13 Novembre 1782
615 *et* 616 *deux de* -	30 - }	—— *Robert Pedley* - - - -	—— 6 Octobre - 1783
617 *et* 618 *deux de* - -	20 - }		
938 *à* 942 *cinq de* - -	20 -	—— *Thomas Coker* - - - -	—— 25 Novembre 1783
499 - - - - - - -	50 -	—— *Samuel Vaughan* - - -	—— 20 Avril - - 1784
1012 - - - - - - - -	50 -	—— *Le Capitaine John Burville*	—— 16 Aout - - 1785
1556 *et* 1557 *deux de* -	30 - }	—— *Milady St. George* - -	—— 21 Octobre - 1785
1558 *et* 1559 *deux de* -	20 - }		
4006 *et* 4007 *deux de* -	20 -	—— *James Trevenen* - - -	—— 4 Janvier - - 1785
1694 - - - - - - - -	100 -	—— *Milord Vicomte Downe*	—— 8 Novembre 1785
1810 - - - - - - -	100 -	—— *Idem* - - - - - - - -	—— 22 do. - - - 1785
3234 *et* 3235 *deux de* -	50 - ⎫		
3236 - - - - - - - -	30 - ⎬ —— *Charles Grey* - - - - -		—— 13 Juin - - - 1786
3237 *et* 3238 *deux de* -	20 - ⎪		
3239 - - - - - - -	30 - ⎭		
3943 *et* 3944 *deux de* -	25 -	—— *Le Chev. J. Gregory Shaw*	—— 11 Aout - - 1786
3969 - - - - - - -	50 -	—— *Daniel Bergman* - - -	—— 15 do. - - - 1786
4109 - - - - - - -	25 - }	—— *Milord Comte de Craufurd*	—— 29 do. - - - 1786
4110 *et* 4111 *deux de* -	20 - }		
5322 *et* 5325 *deux de* -	30 - }	—— *Le Capit. Henry Greville*	—— 29 Juillet - 1788
5329 - - - - - - -	20 - }		
4010 *et* 4011 *deux de* -	40 - ⎫		
4014 *et* 4015 *deux de* -	30 - ⎬ —— *Le General West Hyde*		—— 8 Aout - - 1789
4017 *à* 4019 *trois de* -	20 - ⎭		
4228 *et* 4229 *deux de* -	20 -	—— *William Parsons* - - -	—— 28 Avril - - 1791
4528 - - - - - - - -	50 -	—— *M. de Calonne* - - - -	—— 27 Mai - - 1791
6007 - - - - - - - -	30 -	—— *Joseph Carpenter* - - -	—— 3 Aout - - 1791
3272 *à* 3275 *quatre de* -	20 -	—— *Le Capitaine W. Bentinck*	—— 10 Mars - - 1792
3730 *et* 3731 *deux de* -	50 - ⎫		
3732 *et* 3733 *deux de* -	30 - ⎬ —— *William Tait* - - - - -		—— 27 Avril - - 1792
3734 *et* 3735 *deux de* -	20 - ⎭		
6393 - - - - - - - -	24 18 }	—— *Thomas Cuninghame* -	—— 13 Novembre 1792
6394 *à* 639' *trois de* -	25 - }		
6688 *à* 6692 *cinq de* -	100 -	—— *Richard Wynne* - - - -	—— 21 Decembre 1792

A list of circular notes lost or gone astray between 1781 and 1792, with names of people to whom they had been issued. Herries asks his correspondents not to make payments. A covering letter of 19 April 1793 puts some of the blame on postal disruption in France, implying that tourists themselves were not necessarily to blame

It is charitable, though no doubt naïve, to see this story as another example of the honesty of common people in Europe towards the tourist, which contrasts with an almost institutionalized swindling in accommodation and horse hire. There are so many anecdotes about honesty throughout the later years of the Grand Tour that the overall picture cannot be dismissed. Aiton, for instance, tells of an anxious Scottish clergyman who arrived after dark in a poor suburb of Vienna. He urgently needed the right money for his postilion and had no option but to give a gold coin worth eight shillings to a street urchin who was to procure change. A few minutes later the boy panted back with a handful of cash. The postilion took what he said belonged to him and when the cleric had a chance later to audit his accounts, with local help, he found everything correct to a farthing.[61]

Other stories are equally cheering. In 1819 H. Matthews had breakfast in a café in Milan, before touring the town. Some hours afterwards he realized his purse, containing some 70 Napoleons, was missing. Remembering he had used it at the café, he raced back, convincing himself of 'the knavish expression' of the waiter. As he entered, however, the man sprang forward, purse in hand, saying '*Ecco, Signore!*'[62] In 1840 Catherine Sedgwick, an American lady, left her purse overnight on railings in Wiesbaden. It was found, given to the police, and returned to the owner. The finder and police declined a reward.[63] In short, travellers seem to have been very fairly treated as long as their monetary dealings with Europeans were not in a one-to-one business relationship.

With the Peace of Amiens, effective from 25 March 1802, the British once again rushed abroad, impatient to find out what had happened in France. Unfortunately, war broke out again on 18 May 1803 and about one thousand Britons were trapped across the Channel and interned, many until the end of the war. Obviously, there had been little scope in this brief interval to re-promote circular notes, but the new firm of Herries, Farquhar & Co. survived well enough on the strength of its ancillary business as a West End banking house.

The abdication of Napoleon in April 1814 was the signal for English travellers to desert their land with the enthusiasm of boys leaving boarding school at the end of term. Herries, Farquhar immediately re-established its arrangements, and circular notes to the value of over £21,000 were issued before the end of the month, compared with only £460 worth throughout March.[64] Ironically, the total value of notes issued in 1814 (£96,000) was more than in 1815 (£72,750). The only really busy month for notes in 1815 was July (the month after Waterloo); after then travellers found the French, in the ignominy of defeat, more resentful towards the British than they had been earlier in the year. But the padlocks were off Europe, momentum was established, and more than £153,000 worth of circular notes were issued in 1816. By 1819 issues had peaked at around £244,000, a total not surpassed until 1845.[65]

Appendix Two is a graph of circular note issues for the years between 1814 and 1860. It is noticeable that the European revolutions of 1848

Signatures of the poet Percy Bysshe Shelley (1792–1822) and his wife Harriet in the records of Call, Marten & Co., private bankers of Bond Street, London. (This firm amalgamated in 1865 with Herries, Farquhar & Co.) The date is 9 July 1814: nineteen days later Shelley eloped to France and Switzerland with Mary Godwin, no doubt provided with circular notes from his newly acquired bankers. In December 1816 Harriet committed suicide, drowning in London's Serpentine

caused a marked down-turn in issues, as had the troubles in France in 1830 when Charles X was overthrown. In fact, the issue of circular notes can be seen as a barometer of political tensions in Europe. The graph also shows that the level of popularity of the transferable note, which in some respects was the last non-commercial expression of the bill of exchange, fell away to extinction.

To accompany the post-1815 renaissance of Europe came a new brand of guidebook and 'hints for travellers'. Authors drew attention to the virtues of circular notes, but in prosaic terms lifted directly from their banker's prospectus. In this way Herries, Farquhar & Co. had some lacklustre publicity, but so did Hammersley, and Ransom & Morland; furthermore the supply of circular letters of credit, for which demand remained strong, was often attributed to Messrs Coutts. But soon no banker could feel complacent about his share of the tourist's credit as guidebooks were also pointing out alternative sources of money supply. For the normal journey from Calais to Paris it was possible to buy French money from Messrs Solomon in New Street, Covent Garden; or from Smart in Prince's Street, Leicester Square; or from Thomas in Cornhill, in the City.[66] It was also possible to exchange English money in Paris at the Palais Royal which, since the Revolution, had turned from fashionable rendezvous to a complex of restaurants, brothels and shops, with at least three men running what would now be called *bureaux de change*.[67]

So much for the issue of circular notes, and their recommendation. It is now necessary to look at them from the traveller's viewpoint and study first-hand impressions. Unfortunately, the level of recorded reaction in the eighteenth century appears to be minimal, perhaps indicating that Herries made little headway with his innovation before the French Wars. The situation after 1815 is significantly clearer. If Byron is typical of travellers in the immediate post-war years, then they used more than one form of money order, with circular notes well to the fore. Byron kept a good stock of such notes, the equivalent of a year's supply of money. One advantage of them (which Herries had never publicized), was that the longer term expatriate could use them to play the money market. For instance, Byron wrote from Genoa in April 1823 to his friend Douglas Kinnaird: 'I am about as the Exchange is high (*very* high) to convert several of my circulars into monies of the Country'. A few days later, he wrote again: 'I have also a thousand in Circulars still – fifteen hundred I converted the other day as the exchange was temptingly in favour – and at the same time likely to alter'. Byron's circular notes, from Ransom & Morland's bank, were supplemented by letters of credit for proposed journeys as far as the Levant.[68]

Naples, the most southerly place in mainland Italy where travellers could encash one of Herries's circular notes. The island of Capri is seen at the entrance to the harbour

References to circular notes become quite common in tourists' memoirs from the 1820s. J. Holman can be mentioned who, in Montpellier, acquired 'a fresh supply of Herries and Farquhar's notes, from my punctual and obliging banker in London. . . . I shall avail myself of this opportunity of recommending to travellers the superior advantages of Herries and Farquhar's notes, in preference to letters of credit. . . .'[69] He then paraphrases the prospectus. Although it is probable that Herries, Farquhar & Co. retained the lion's share of note issue, Robert Herries would have been disconsolate that the increasing publicity for his rivals was not confined to the writers of guidebooks. E. Spencer, for instance, in 1836, advocated from experience the 'circular bills of the Messrs Hammersleys' whose agents he 'always found to be highly respectable men'.[70] And when Herries, Farquhar & Co. did get publicity it was not necessarily to their liking:

Should you apply to Herries for some of their circular billets, just give my compliments, and inquire how it is that neither theirs, nor those of other bankers, can ever be sold to any of their numerous correspondents without further deductions being made under various pretexts, beyond what they lead you to suppose, even when payment is required in the common coin of the country, and not in any coin that bears a premium. A good many of us abroad would be glad to be enlightened upon this point, and if properly explained, it may save . . . travellers an equal share of vexation and disappointment, in quarters where they have no right to expect it.[71]

That was the view of H.J. Whitling, and his criticism demolished one of the corner-stones of Robert Herries's original argument. As Herries himself would never have stood for it, this is likely to have been a drawback which evolved after the interval of the French Wars. The partnership then was not unaware of this problem, among 'various complaints', but thought little could be done about it. The firm simply reiterated that its instructions to correspondents were positive and regretted a 'too general . . . disposition to make a paltry advantage on English travellers which we should have hoped any House of the least character would consider beneath them . . .'.[72] As this statement was in 1815, and Whitling wrote in 1844, clearly their faith in human nature was unfounded. The character of other complaints is not known, except that some tourists found that denominations of circular notes were too high. Aiton, for instance, claimed that the minimum sum for a circular note was £100, although it could be negotiated in units down to £20.[73] However, notes from £10 upwards were found in the 1870s.

Such evidence of imperfection should not put our judgment of the scheme out of balance. It is possible to believe that circular notes were routine and satisfactory for more than 90 per cent of travellers, who therefore had no reason to mention them. An interesting pointer to the status of circular notes is provided by J.F. Campbell, a self-styled 'briefless barrister', writing in 1876. Campbell had just travelled round the world, and entitled his reminiscences *My Circular Notes*. These were prefaced by a drawing of a 'skit' note and by a 'Letter of Introduction', parodying the name, if not the content, of the traveller's letter of order.[74]

As Campbell made minimal reference to circular notes in the book itself, the title signifies that the concept and use of the notes were well enough known for his puns to be understood without further explanation. In fact it is likely that by then no other form of money order was in anything like common use. Murray's *European Handbooks* now contained such phrases as: 'A very safe method of carrying money is by circular notes issued by Coutts & Co., Herries & Co., the London & Westminster Bank, and other banks'.[75] As the London & Westminster was a joint-stock bank, as opposed to a private bank, competition for the issue

MY CIRCULAR NOTES.

Mess.ᵣˢ Stewards, Boots & Cᵒ
£10000„0„0:
  Pay bearer, on demand,
Ten thousand Pounds Sterling,
value received,
£10000„0„0:   H. Walker & Co

LETTER OF INTRODUCTION.

July 26, 1875.

The mental matters upon the following pages were dressed in paper between this date and July 6, 1874. The writer on these papers—a briefless barrister, and public servant out of place, "took the world for his pillow," like the lad in the story, and set out to amuse himself in that long vacation which he hopes will last for many years, and his life. He might have been wearing out arm-chairs in London, well-paid and housed for doing very little; he prefers to please himself, and ramble with some object in view. "It's better to wear shoon than sheets," according to the old saw; "It's better to hear the lark sing

VOL. I.   **B**

The opening of the first volume of the travel book *My Circular Notes*, written by the 'briefless barrister' J.F. Campbell and published in 1876. As well as referring to the circular note system in the title, Campbell reproduces a stylized note parodying the traveller's continuous payments to 'stewards' and 'boots' [hotel pages]. The allusion to travel papers is carried even further by the phrase 'Letter of Introduction'

of notes was clearly becoming intense. There was still a market for circular letters of credit, but these were being issued mainly to representatives of commercial houses, while the bill of exchange had reverted to its role as an instrument of business.

There is, nevertheless, some evidence of Bank of England seven-day post bills being used as an alternative form of remittance to people domiciled abroad.[76] Technically, these were somewhere between a bill of exchange and a promissory note and were issued only by the Bank of England, but not necessarily in London as by the mid-nineteenth century the bank had several country branches. Payable seven days after sight, these bills could be 'accepted' or 'unaccepted' at the time of issue, and were available to private individuals; in those days it was possible for well-heeled people to have an account with the Bank of England as they might otherwise have done with a local private bank, or branch of a banking company.

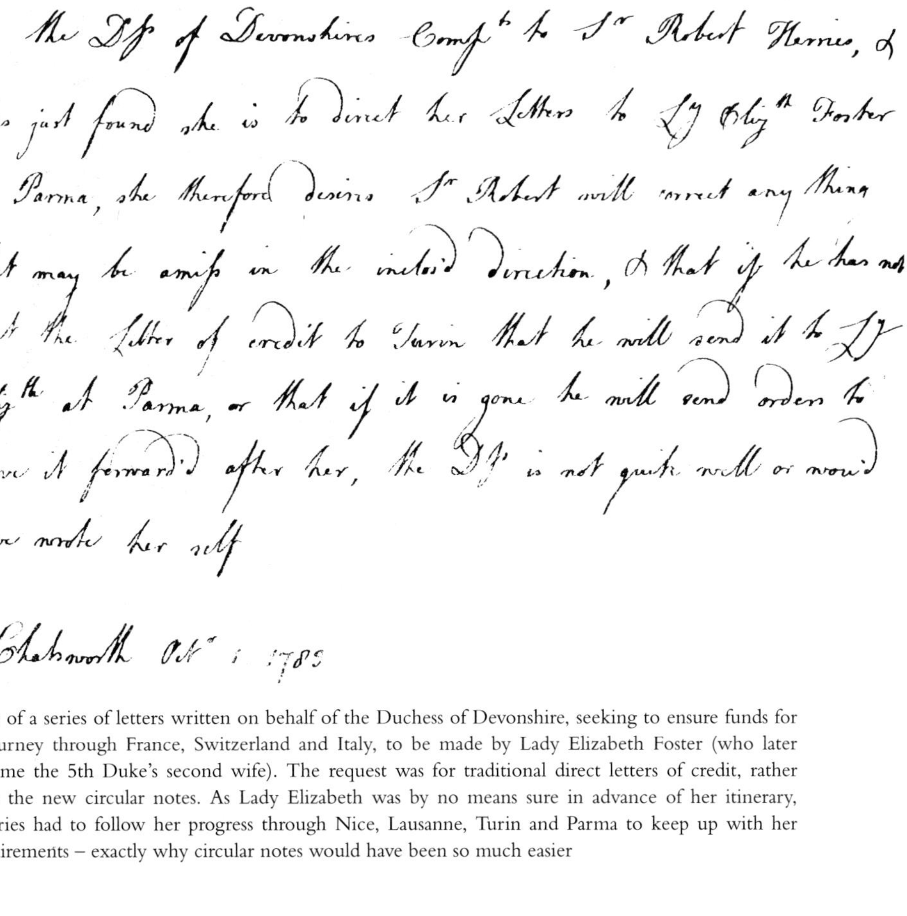

[handwritten letter, reproduced as an image]

The D[uche]ss of Devonshire Comp[limen]ts to S[i]r Robert Herries, & has just found she is to direct her Letters to L[ad]y Eliz[abe]th Foster to Parma, she therefore desires S[i]r Robert will correct any thing that may be amiss in the inclos'd direction, & that if he has not sent the Letter of credit to Turin that he will send it to L[ad]y Eliz[abe]th at Parma, or that if it is gone he will send orders to have it forward'd after her, the D[uche]ss is not quite well or wou'd have wrote her self

Chatsworth Oct[obe]r ? 1785

One of a series of letters written on behalf of the Duchess of Devonshire, seeking to ensure funds for a journey through France, Switzerland and Italy, to be made by Lady Elizabeth Foster (who later became the 5th Duke's second wife). The request was for traditional direct letters of credit, rather than the new circular notes. As Lady Elizabeth was by no means sure in advance of her itinerary, Herries had to follow her progress through Nice, Lausanne, Turin and Parma to keep up with her requirements – exactly why circular notes would have been so much easier

The only serious alternative, however, to circular notes was gold, which made something of a comeback in the safer conditions of travel of the later nineteenth century. One of Campbell's fellow Britons on the ship to North America had £4,000 worth about his person; Campbell thought him a fool but he himself had £200 in gold for emergencies.[77] It is from the 1830s that we find increasing evidence of English sovereigns becoming acceptable in northern Europe, and Aiton recommended gold for Germany in 1842 as better than any kind of money order.[78] That was apparently not the case in parts of France. C.R. Weld, a visitor to Clermont Ferrand in 1850, found that his hotel keeper would not take English gold at all. At a local bank he could only get 23 francs for a sovereign when the published course of exchange, lying in front of both of them on the banker's table, was 25 francs and 40 cents. Weld walked out in disgust, pursued a little later by the banker's clerk, now offering 23 francs and 50 cents.[79]

As for English banknotes, there was quite a difference of opinion. In north Europe Spencer thought they were 'never advisable', being only acceptable to bankers in German ports.[80] Aiton, however, was assured that English banknotes would be received in all the larger towns.[81] By the 1860s, when Thomas Cook was organizing his excursions to France, Switzerland and Italy, Bank of England notes were widely acceptable. Before Cook is looked at in more detail, however, the increasing popularity in Europe of the decimal system must be realized. In France the franc had been introduced in 1799 and the old currency, based on the livre (Tournois), ceased to be legal tender in 1834. There were 20 franc pieces of gold, called Napoleons or Louis d'ors, and other gold coins for denominations of 100, 50, 10 and 5 francs. The English sovereign and £1 note were usually exchanged for 25 francs, but the tourist had to be on guard that he was not given Napoleons instead. The major advance, however, was in 1865, when a Latin Monetary Union was formed between France, Italy, Belgium and Switzerland, who were joined by Greece in 1868. These countries adopted the same unit of value, although called by different names (i.e. franc, lira, and drachma) and their gold coins were interchangeable. The union survived until after the First World War, with many other European countries adopting the system, without acceding to membership.[82]

Such sophistication of practice is a reminder that this story is about to leave behind the world of foreign travel as Robert Herries had known it. But before it does so, another look must be taken at the role of banker as travel agent which was seen developing in the last chapter. As already stated, Herries thought the circular note would free the European banker

from the social obligations which came his way, whether or not he liked
them. In fact it did not. Any form of recommendation from one banker
to another, whether by letters of credit or less pointedly by circular notes,
attracted much the same level of personal attention. No doubt if C.R.
Weld, mentioned above, had gone to the local banker in Clermont
Ferrand with some personal recommendation, he would not have been
short-changed, and might have had a glass of good wine into the bargain.
Nor would the traveller David Ricardo have met with his experience at
Lyons, where he arrived in 1822:

> I was without credit and unknown. I endeavoured to get money from
> a banker here by a display of my Passport, which gave me my most
> distinguishing title; a letter with some complimentary expressions of
> their confidence in me from Messrs Delessert; and lastly certificates of
> a large sum of French Stock being in my name; but without success –
> they would not give me a shilling – My good natured landlord came
> to my relief . . . and advanced me 2,000 francs which I am to repay
> in Paris.[83]

Whatever had been the beliefs of its founder, the firm of Herries,
Farquhar & Co. realized that circular notes were no check to the banker-
customer social relationship as it was still evolving. The notes themselves
were irrelevant to the process; it was the letter of order which counted.
By 1815 this letter, wrote Herries, Farquhar & Co., 'whilst it serves to
identify, also gives the Traveller a claim to any attentions or good offices
that he may stand in need of'.[84] This was the reassurance that circular
notes attracted the same perks as letters of credit. For by now tourists were
so pampered by their European bankers that few would have swapped a
more efficient form of money order for a less comprehensive service at
the level of friend and counsellor.

The French Wars, despite the disruption they caused to the mechanics
of money transmission, did nothing to stop the almost sycophantic
dedication of continental bankers to the comfort of *milord anglais*, his wife,
or his offspring. Traditions of service descended through generations of
bankers' families. The firm of Hentsch at Geneva is particularly well
remembered in diaries throughout the period of the Grand Tour.[85] Father
and son took vicarious enjoyment from the satisfaction of their clients and
agonized in their distress when things went wrong. Sometimes the
indebtedness of traveller, parent or sponsor could never adequately be
repaid. The following incident of the Philips boys is a case in point.

Geneva, although a relatively small city, was probably the most visited and popular stopover on the Grand Tour. Picturesquely situated between the Rivers Rhône and Arve, and Lac Leman (as this early nineteenth-century map indicates), Geneva became a symbol of civil and religious tolerance, despite the dominance of Calvinism since the Reformation. The engraving shows the city from the right bank of the Rhône

In 1798 Geneva was annexed to France, but avoided the worst problems of the war with Britain. When, therefore, an order was issued for all Englishmen aged eighteen or over to be arrested, many travellers, having believed themselves safe, were horrified. Among them was Dr Peter Roget, later to compile the famous *Thesaurus*, but then a twenty-three-year-old governor of two young English tourists, sons of John Philips, a Mancunian merchant. Roget describes the confusion and panic:

> M. Prévost . . . advised us to be off without losing a moment. We did
> not require this advice to be twice given us. We just shook M and Mme
> Peschier [their hosts] by the hand, flew out of the house, ordered horses
> from Moré's to be sent to Voirombé, and were hastening out of the
> town, when we met Mr Ansley, who told us that Edgeworth [their
> friend] was at Mr Hentsch's. Thither I accordingly went, and found a
> large circle of ladies and one gentleman in the counting-house. They
> were talking with great eagerness of the subject of our present alarm.
> The Marchioness of Donegal asked me a few questions relative to it. All
> was in confusion at the counting-house; Mr Hentsch exhibited the
> picture of despair. I took bills of exchange for the money we had with
> him, and we again sallied forth. . . .[86]

It was Charles Hentsch who wrote a reassuring letter to John Philips describing his sons' escape from Geneva.[87] This was presumably at some risk to himself and his firm. Some years later, in a more peaceful climate, Hentsch was very useful to Byron. He sent manuscripts back to England, acted as a clearing house for his letters, and was prepared to find two furnished houses, one for Byron himself and the other for his friends, the Gamba family.[88] This was not the only time Byron used a banker as estate agent. He got Charles Barry, a most cooperative expatriate banker in Genoa, to look out for a house for the Earl of Blessington.[89]

These examples have simply been highlights in a catalogue of services and courtesies which could be indefinitely extended. Bankers were recommended in guidebooks as custodians of valuables if one's innkeeper would not accept temporary deposit of the door key, and with it responsibility for the room in the visitor's absence. When Peter Beckford advised travellers between Florence and Rome to use a *vetturino*, hired by written agreement, he suggested that a banker should see the document was properly drawn up and executed.[90] Also at Florence, it was bankers, not innkeepers, who could arrange for tourists' luggage to be searched where they were staying, rather than at the customs house; and it was

Heidelberg, beautifully situated on the river Neckar and famed for its university, founded in 1386. The print shows the ruined castle, once the residence of the Electors Palatine. Tourists visiting its cellars were shown what was reputedly the largest tun in the world, able to hold eight hundred hogsheads of wine

bankers who had arranged for it to arrive in the first place, often by sea, and the river Arno, direct from Nice. The banker was, of course, no less useful for the traveller himself, on the land journey. It was wise to have letters of introduction, even for a stop-over, as Henry Best discovered at Milan in the early 1820s. 'I wish to stay here a week,' he said to the commissary of police. 'You know some one at Milan? Some banker?' asked the man. 'Not a soul; not even a banker,' replied Best, 'as I have funds with me for my journey to Florence'. He volunteered to leave after three days. Best had later to thank one of his European bankers for acting as a missing persons' bureau. His erstwhile servant, Antoine, by dint of persistent enquiry at Best's Parisian banker's, was reunited with his master to their mutual delight and rejoined his service back in England.[91]

Another use for the banker was as a reference for admission to casinos. These institutions, which developed (particularly in Germany) in the early nineteenth century, were more than gambling houses and were supported by subscriptions from the nobility and bourgeoisie. Often attached to the

Kursaal ('cure-hall') in a watering-place, they included reading rooms with newspapers from several countries, conversation rooms, billiard and card rooms. There were also assembly rooms used for balls, and often a good restaurant. Many travellers were fascinated by casinos, admiring the glamour of the décor, the earnest silence, the rattle of the wheel, and the tinkle of gold. C.E. Dod was awestruck: 'Pretty, interesting women were putting down their Napoleons, and seeing them swept away, or drawing them in doubled, with a sang-froid which proved they were no novices in their employment'.[92] The American Catherine Sedgwick, on the other hand, was as dismayed by the expressionless faces of lady gamblers as she was by the gambling itself, particularly as it was permitted on Sundays.[93]

Bankers had now found their uncertain social position of earlier years was resolved and whether or not they were Jewish was an irrelevance. There was no longer confusion with merchants who, by the middle of the nineteenth century, had lost their involvement with casual tourists. Bankers in larger towns were invariably prosperous, with a social respectability to match. 'When you do not happen to have . . . the advice of some excellent family of your own country,' suggested W. Howitt in 1844, 'take that of the banker who has been recommended to you, whose interest it is to put you right, and who generally belongs to the best class of people'.[94]

British travellers seem too cosseted to have realized what an extraordinary thing it was for bankers to have such a double image: at home they could be tight and assertive; abroad they were sweetness and generosity personified, given the right introduction. It took our American friend, Miss Sedgwick, to point out the peculiarity of the system. Her prestigious little party arrived in Frankfurt in 1840 and dined at the house of Herr Kock, without even a business connection:

> He is an eminent banker here, and from his extensive English connexions, is in some sort compelled to be a general receiver of Continental tourists. We do not bank with him, and therefore have not this claim . . . upon his hospitality; but, for all that, it has been most liberally extended to us. A family whose hospitality is not exhausted in such a thoroughfare as Frankfurt, must have an inexhaustible fountain of humanity. Hospitality in an isolated country residence is the mere gratification of the appetite of a social being; here it is virtue.[95]

But it was not to be a virtue for long. As steam power killed the romance of the Grand Tour, so package holidays distanced the tourist from his foreign banker. In these circumstances, the circular note descended from the heady realms of social excess and continued in the role for which Herries had always intended it – an uncomplicated medium of money supply. As this book is not a history of tourism, there is no time to look too closely at the fascinating story of Thomas Cook, the man who brought about this situation.[96] But the fact is that his excursions were operating to western Europe in the early 1860s, and that traditionalists had no illusions, but that the days of Grand Touring, with all its connotations, were numbered. It was very much a social revolution: travelling was now within the reach of the lower middle class, and the 'old guard' did not like it. Ranged on their side were even some British consuls, remnants of the cohorts of travellers' friends of a century before. The British vice-consul at Spezia, writing in *Blackwood's Edinburgh Magazine* under the pseudonym of Cornelius O'Dowd, incited Cook to publish a rejoinder, full of indignation:

> He, a British Consul, to whom in case of difficulty or emergency I may possibly have to appeal for that protection which is my right, deliberately asserts that he has agreed among the Italians of his acquaintance a report that I am engaged by the Government of this country to take groups of convicts abroad, and, by leaving three or four at each of the different cities I visit, gradually distribute the sweepings of our prison-houses over Europe.[97]

This book will not enter the debate. It is obvious, however, that as package tourism increased dramatically, as was the case, travel became more institutionalized; the special relationship was now between the British tourist and his 'excursion agent' rather than the tourist and his banker. It was not so much that Cook usurped the foreign banker's role; it was more that he made it redundant. True, the firm of Thos Cook & Son had been set up as early as 1841 as 'Bankers and Tourist Agents' but the banking side of it was too insignificant to warrant a place in the annual *Bankers' Almanac* until the 1890s.[98] In the early days there was no question of Cook issuing circular notes. 'To purchasers of tickets in our office in London', he advertised, 'we are generally prepared to supply small amounts of French money'.[99] In 1866 came the introduction of travel vouchers, later developed as a system of coupons which, allied to the firm's own circular notes, gained the tourist wide acceptance at hotels and banks.[100]

But the point about Cook's tours was that the excursionist, having prepaid, could largely forget about the problems of money altogether, except for presents and minor expenses. In this way the market for circular notes diminished somewhat, and for some twenty years from around 1870 they became only a minor service in the expanding portfolio of banking. A nice, forgotten irony is that bank clerks were prominent among the new class of tourist whom Cook introduced to the world at large. History does not record whether their upper-class customers, receiving circular notes for Geneva, Venice or the Rhineland, were treated to a supercilious smirk.

4
BRITAIN AS HOST: MONEY AND TOURISM IN THE BRITISH ISLES

So far this book has looked at travelling abroad, mostly in Europe and through the eyes of Britons. To balance the picture, it must now consider tourism in Britain itself and discover how both foreign and native travellers made provision for their money. This is a necessary step before, in the next chapter, the impact is examined of tourism from North America.

Before the eighteenth century, foreign travellers tended to visit Britain for the same specific motives (academic, religious, diplomatic and commercial) that inspired travellers from Britain to go abroad; although the volume of traffic into Britain was much less than the volume in the other direction. With the accession of the Hanoverians, however, the political climate was conducive for the Germans to visit more casually and more often, while French, Scandinavian and other tourists increasingly ventured beyond London for the same miscellany of reasons and incentives which prompted the British to travel on the Grand Tour. It also became fashionable and instructive for Britons to travel through their own land, reporting on antiquities, curiosities, burgeoning industrial growth and agricultural improvement.

It follows that if the Grand Tour is regarded as a pan-European phenomenon, Britain was as much a part of the itinerary as anywhere else. However, the searching of diaries and memoirs for evidence of travellers' money supply in Britain is as exhausting as the same exercise for British travellers on the Continent. And even this scant information is more forthcoming than evidence of how the British got by in their own country. In a sense this situation mirrors the wider aspects of domestic travel. For many centuries there was little communication between urban centres, unless of necessity. By-roads were unexplored. It was possible to find communities in the same county as remote from each other as their county town was from London. When William Camden approached

Lancashire from Yorkshire 'with a kind of aversion' at the turn of the sixteenth century, he described it as settled by 'Brigantes . . . beyond the mountains towards the Western ocean'. He hoped this was not an omen of 'ill success'.[1] Such cautious, unknowing words seem more suited to the era of Julius Caesar. Certainly hopes of finding anything as civilized as a country bank would not have crossed the traveller's mind until the second half of the eighteenth century.

The impression created by diarists, like Celia Fiennes (beginning her tours through Britain in about 1685), is that the need for periodic injections of money was somehow non-existent. In her case at least this was thanks to a national network of relations and a convention among landowners that a strange gentlewoman and her two maidservants were entitled to free board and lodging as a matter of civility. Finding themselves, for instance, three miles short of Daventry on the rough road from Warwick, Celia and her companions were plucked from the slough of a disagreeable village by Lord and Lady Shuckburgh who, living nearby, 'very curteously tooke compassion on us and treated us very handsomly that night, a good supper serv'd in plaite and very good wine, and good beds . . .'.[2] But now and again inns were unavoidable for Celia, and the initial supply of money had surely run out. It is not clear whether she had a very businesslike arrangement with bills of exchange at the houses of those of her relations who were also merchants, or a very unbusinesslike arrangement within the family as a whole, whereby she was given or lent money on demand.

For foreign visitors to Britain such casual, if effective, arrangements were out of the question. With due regard for the difficulties of exporting specie, which has already been discussed, the choice was between buying ready money in England at the normal rate of exchange, or taking bills of exchange, or letters of credit. These were, of course, very much the options open to Englishmen who travelled in the opposite direction. The strong trading links between Britain and Europe made it particularly easy to deposit local money with a merchant in Hamburg, or Rotterdam, or Antwerp, and arrange to draw up to the sterling equivalent of that sum at the office of his London correspondent. The real debt was then just another book transaction in the ordinary course of international business between merchants. When such a facility could not be arranged, or when a foreigner's arrival in London anticipated the note of credit on his behalf, the changing of continental coin was normally to the traveller's disadvantage.[3] Such exchange could be effected at the house of a goldsmith in Lombard Street, or at the offices of a silversmith or money changer, some of whom worked above the Bank of England. This was in the early period (1695–1734) when the bank occupied Grocers' Hall in Poultry. It appears from the travel diary of Zacharias Conrad von Uffenbach, visiting London in 1710, that these men would also discount bills of exchange, enabling the visitor to get at his money, less a small deduction, before he was due to receive it from a mercantile house.[4]

Having crossed the Channel, tourists were immediately intrigued by British money which, under the Tudors, became of relatively high quality. When Thomas Platter visited London from Basel in 1599, he complimented the Crown for minting coins only of pure gold and silver, the lowest denomination being the tiny silver halfpenny. 'If one buys to the value of less than a half-penny,' reported Platter, 'permission is granted

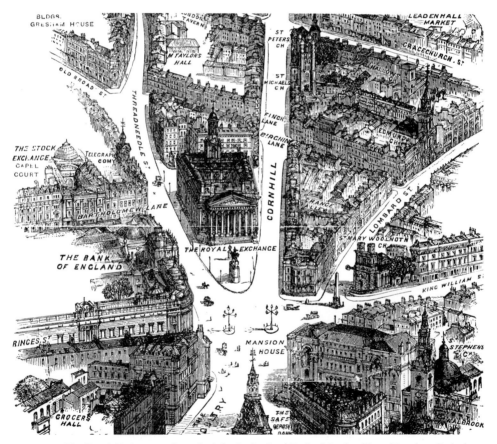

The Royal Exchange and, to the left, the Bank of England in the City of London. Both these commercial centres attracted as many foreign tourists as the more obvious landmarks. The Bank, especially, had a reputation for tolerance and courtesy in the reception of visitors

to mint lead or copper symbols in one's own house, some 4 or 6 going to a halfpenny, and these symbols are given to the apprentices; when they have a halfpenny worth or more, they exchange and reckon up together so that nobody loses.'[5] This was a far cry from parts of Europe where the debasement of national coinage was a perk of supreme authority. Unfortunately, the high standard of British coinage was not maintained by the Stuarts.

When money, *per se*, lost its charm, fascination transferred to the scale on which banking was conducted, in particular by the Bank of England which had moved to purpose-built premises in Threadneedle Street in 1735. For more than two centuries the bank adopted a tolerant attitude to the gaze and dawdle of foreign tourists; much of their inspection and admiration was architectural, for the bank as a building type was scarcely known abroad. There was equal interest in the Royal Mint, where the production of money was a literal end-product of the technology and mystique of the Industrial Revolution. We have already noticed this attraction abroad, and the drama of stamp and die was no less mesmeric in London and Dublin than in Milan and St Petersburg.

If there were similarities with the Continent in that respect, the greater degree of organization and cohesion in London banking cast a spell all of its own. Many tourists were puzzled, and indeed impressed, by the relaxed attitudes of bankers and their clerks. One visitor, in 1810, had been expecting that with a credit of £1,000 waved in his banker's face he would 'appear a considerable personage; but, on entering his counting-house all your greatness sinks into dust. Fifty, sixty, and more clerks you see busied around, whole hills of bank-notes you behold heaped up . . .'.[6] A decade later, at the Bank of England, Prince Pückler-Muskau found himself 'gaping at the heaps of gold and casks of silver which seem to . . . bring to life the treasures of the Arabian Nights'.[7]

The best testimony to the spectacle of London banking is offered by a Frenchman, Francis Wey. Although as late as 1856, the date merely demonstrates that nothing had changed. He strolled around the City, looking at banks, and wondering where the sentries and troops were. He found he could saunter in and out and open doors. Cashiers sat at low tables with no iron railings, shovelling up gold as a grocer ladles salt or rice. In one bank he was invited to inspect an 8 lb nugget of gold. 'When I had examined it I handed it to my neighbour who passed it on to his, and from hand to hand it disappeared down the passage which gave out on to the street. The clerk took no further notice of it, talked of other things, and when it reappeared took it, not only without the slightest show of relief but as though he had forgotten its very existence.'[8]

It is no matter that this picture of complacency conflicts with the image of London banking as its Victorian practitioners have led us to understand it; the point is made that foreigners recognized differences in style, custom and practice, evoking admiration in some and wonderment in most. Away from London, however, the evolving complications of country banking, rooted in the origins and aftermath of the Industrial Revolution, hardly impinged at all on the tourist throughout the eighteenth century. Typically, he had exchange arrangements only in London and used the capital as a base for excursions lasting no longer than the duration of his money supply.

Those who travelled further afield are characteristically coy in revealing their credit arrangements. No doubt they were intrigued by the variety of local bankers – plump and eccentric like 'Jemmy' Wood at Gloucester, lean and austere like the Quakers, or aloof and smart in the larger cities. The absence of Jews would have surprised them. Even more bewildering were some of banking's ancillary workers. In 1809 the Dane A.A. Feldborg (writing as J.A. Andersen) published his memoirs of an excursion through Britain. At Berwick-on-Tweed, peaceably eating at an inn, he was amazed at the intrusion of a bulky, rolling young man who 'bounced up to my table . . . rubbing his hands, and without further ceremony said, So, Sir! you are taking a lunch!' The youth then turned away, accosted someone else, and vanished. Minutes later he reappeared, emptying wallet and pockets of paper while denouncing a local bank 'which would not give him a bill on London for a large sum, at a shorter date than forty days'.[9] This colourful fellow was a London rider, one of the essential links between the metropolitan and provincial banking systems.

Eccentricities aside, Feldborg's experience gives us an immediate insight into the tourist's problem. If he took bills of exchange in London, from his merchant contact or banker, payable at the office of a country correspondent, he had to wait a considerable time for the maturity date: assuming that the normal business terms of thirty or sixty days might be reduced in a less commercial context, there was still no safe way of effecting an instant transfer of money. It was *possible* to carry bills of exchange payable on demand (in modern parlance, cheques) but the dangers of highway robbery argued against it. The best which could be hoped for was money seven days after date or sight. This arrangement was introduced in the form of so-called post bills by the Bank of England, and later by other banks, with security in mind; if bills were stolen, this was the minimum safe time in which to cancel payment and apprehend those

The bank of James ('Jemmy') Wood in Westgate Street, Gloucester, with the proprietor in the doorway. Wood, a most wealthy man, represented the eccentric side of English country banking. The business had been founded by his grandfather as early as 1716. Jemmy was 'unmarried; entertained no company; visited no one; spent his whole time in his bank . . . and his Sundays in a long walk in the country'. After he died in 1836 his estate was fiercely contested

who attempted to present them. The original idea, in 1728, had been for three-day post bills, but these failed to gain public confidence and seven-day post bills were introduced in 1738.[10]

This, then, was the position which taxed the mind of Sir Robert Herries after the launch of his circular notes, and other forms of credit, for the Grand Tourist on the mainland of Europe. The fact that in practice an Englishman abroad could now receive his money on demand at provincial centres, but a foreigner (or Englishman) in England could not, was anomalous, frustrating, and intractable. It was not simply a question of security. The real problem was that any provision intended for tourists might have a wider commercial application, thus threatening the vested interests of banks which were already issuing seven-day post bills to facilitate the remittance of money between the provinces and London. Any move by Herries to introduce an instrument payable at shorter date would receive vigorous opposition from those who remembered his earlier move – by some judged surreptitious – into the realms of banking after the introduction of the circular note. As the use and promotion of any kind of bill at shorter date was impossible without the co-operation of correspondent bankers (agents), and as the material risks were anyway very great, there was no possibility of Herries undercutting the accepted period, however much he might have wished it.

Many documents survive to reveal Herries's strategy but most are undated and the chronology of events is by no means clear. As he was already knighted when he first announced (at the foot of an advertisement for circular notes) his own version of inland post bills for Great Britain and Ireland, the date cannot be earlier than 1774. On the other hand it is unlikely to be much later. The wording of the announcement is interesting: the English text states clearly that the idea suggested itself following the success of foreign business, while the French version draws attention to the dangers of highway robbery ('aux vols, trop fréquens, dans les grand chemins') and mentions that Herries & Co. 'ont étés solicités' to establish at home something similar to the circular note scheme.[11]

The earliest printed plan for inland 'Circular Post Bills' and letters of credit is again undated, but likely to have been drafted by Herries in around 1780. The preamble records that this scheme was 'first intended as a branch of the business of his house, but since resolved to be a separate concern of his own'.[12] Why this short-lived change of heart came about is not recorded, but it was typical of Herries, the entrepreneur, to keep a potentially exciting idea under his own wing, particularly as his private involvement with the French tobacco commission had ended, leaving him with something of a void.

The bones of the scheme followed very much the plan for circular notes. The traveller purchased a supply of post bills from Herries and presented them at any of the firms listed, under towns, in the letter of order. In so doing, promised Herries, 'the possessor will at all rates receive the ordinary marks of civility shewn to strangers'[13] – a much less robust assurance than the welcome promised to British travellers at banks on the mainland of Europe. As for the letters of credit, these were either circular or direct and worked as they did abroad: the latter were payable at a given place, the former could be encashed in whole or in part among Herries's correspondents. But whereas circular post bills were subject to no charge, except stamp duty, commission of $\frac{1}{2}$ per cent was paid on letters of credit at the place(s) of payment, and on the recovery of the value in London. The money given by the correspondent to the customer was reclaimed from Herries by a draft – the word used for an instrument of payment drawn between bankers.

Those, at least, were the arrangements as presented to customers. To his prospective correspondents Herries had rather more to say. It was very important, to realize adequate profits, that the post bills themselves should have a wider, longer and more productive life than European circular notes. Whereas the latter were of no value once the traveller had encashed them, and merely returned to Herries in course of post, the new bills could be reused, by endorsement, and negotiated like bills of exchange for other commercial purposes. More important still in Herries's eyes was the remittance business to the capital. Stewards of manors and agents of estates throughout the country, including Scotland and Ireland, needed to send proceeds to absentee landowners, often resident in London. As cash was bulky, heavy, and vulnerable to theft, remitters used it locally to buy good bills on London from bankers, merchants or brokers, which could be sent to the landowners, wherever they might be, for payment at maturity. But the latter had to wait a long time for their money, and even at maturity payment of a bill could be extended by three days of grace.[14]

As bank post bills attracted no such extension, and were at any rate payable after only seven days, Herries's idea was that his correspondents would send him receipts, yearly or half-yearly, for the estate money lodged with them, and that he, having had the receipts, would issue landowners with seven-day post bills. In this way they could touch their money several weeks earlier than before. Money paid in to correspondents in Scotland or Ireland was regulated by Herries according to the printed course of exchange on those centres, with no charge or deduction to the landowner. Thus the bills could have a tourist connotation on their way out to the country and a business connotation on their way back; and could be used commercially by Herries himself within London.[15]

He paid commission to his correspondents for sums paid by them to holders of post bills, tourists or otherwise, and himself received 3 per cent per annum commission from his correspondents on rent moneys etc lodged with them. He likewise allowed 3 per cent to landowners who were prepared to accept a delay in receiving their money, perhaps 'to wait a little for the fall of Stocks or for eligible Mortgages', so profit margins were small. Herries prided himself on the evolution of a system of bills essentially more profitable to the user than the inventor: in his own words, 'the gain though reasonable, will not be equal to the savings and convenience of those who make use of them'. In essence his post bills were not innovations in the paperwork of credit (as had been his circular notes) but represented new ideas in how post bills might be used.[16]

The scheme was to have built-in safeguards against robbery and forgery. The traveller was to write his own name in the second line of the letter of order, although a thief would believe it had been written by a bank clerk. This would provide a specimen signature when the bill was encashed. As for the bills themselves, the paper used was to be similar to that for circular notes, with various flourishes and curiosities (such as a reversed '4' in the top left-hand corner, three kinds of lettering, and three types of ink). Also, the bills were to be cut at each end 'by a particular contrivance'; correspondents were sent specimen counterparts, 'stiffened for the purpose of lasting the longer', which would lodge exactly in the shape of the cuts. When letters of credit, circular and/or direct, were given to travellers without post bills, there was (unusually) no letter of order to be issued, signatures of clients being 'sent by post on slips of paper, along with the advice of the credits and directions for reimbursement'.[17]

In the established bill market of the eighteenth century, Herries was wise to promote his scheme with caution. The idea, he confessed, 'though capable of great extension, is intended to be confined to narrow bounds' at least until its advantages, and conveniency, should be proven by experience. He claimed to be creating a business divested 'of everything like interference with any other existing', except his own circular notes, but obviously his post bills were seen as a threat by others interested in the remittance business. If resentment was inevitable, he hoped that it might at least be minimal, given 'the diminutive way, in which I wish for my own sake to make the experiment'. That sanguine clause was written 'above fifteen years' since the introduction of circular notes, therefore around 1784.[18]

CIRCULAR LETTER OF CREDIT

NORTHERN BANKING COMPANY
LIMITED.
ESTABLISHED 1824.   CABLE ADDRESS, "NORBANK, BELFAST"

BELFAST,
IRELAND,

No. 00000   19

To Messieurs the Bankers named in our list of Correspondents.

Gentlemen, This letter will be presented to you by

who is hereby authorised to draw at sight on Lloyds Bank Ltd., 72 Lombard Street, London, at any time within months from this date to an extent not exceeding (say pounds sterling).

Each draft must be in British currency, must state that it is drawn under Circular Letter of Credit of the Northern Banking Co. Ltd. No. 00000 issued the day of 19 and must be signed in presence of one of your officials by the Accredited, to the accompanying specimen of whose signature we ask your particular attention.

The date and amount of each draft, with the name and address of the Bank negotiating it, must be endorsed hereon, and when the amount of the credit is exhausted this letter must be cancelled and attached to the last draft.

We undertake that drafts so drawn in conformity with this Letter of Credit shall be honored on presentation, and we request that you negotiate them at current rate for sight drafts on London, collecting your charges, if any, from the Bearer hereof.

Asking for your usual courtesies.

We are, Gentlemen, Your obedient servants,

per pro. Northern Banking Co. Ltd.

SEE BACK.

A circular letter of credit, to be endorsed with details of withdrawals to the stated sum, was available as an option for tourists as late as the 1950s. Their main drawback (apart from being too large for most wallets), was that they were intended simply as a means to acquire foreign money; they were no use in settling an hotel bill

THOMAS COUTTS, ESQ:

Died Feb. 24, 1822. Aged 87.

Published March.1822. by John Fairburn.Broadway, Ludgate Hill.

The famous banker Thomas Coutts (1735–1822), responsible for issuing his firm's circular notes in opposition to those of Robert Herries. He became sole partner of the family's London banking-house in 1778. Ten years later, he and his family embarked on their own Grand Tour of Europe

In contrast to 'Jemmy' Wood at Gloucester (see p. 83), there were some very smart and personable provincial bankers in England, especially in the major ports, where competition was fiercest. This Liverpool private banker, a natty dresser, looks very comfortable against the elegant backdrop of his city's exchange

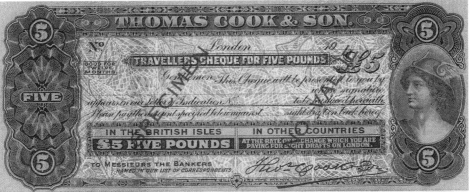

Traveller's cheques issued by Thomas Cook & Son, and by their banking arm Thos. Cook & Son (Bankers) Ltd, earlier this century. Note that the American version reads 'Travelers' but, perhaps surprisingly, 'Cheque', not 'Check'

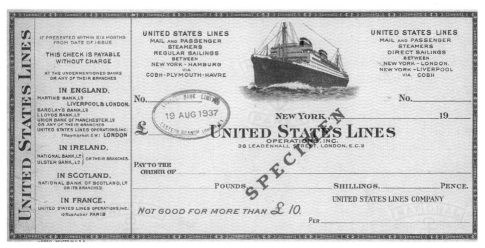

Among shipping companies which issued their own sterling traveller's cheques was the United States Line, rivals to Cunard on the lucrative routes between New York and Europe

Lloyds Bank traveller's cheques for £5 and £10, encashed in 1928

Traveller's cheques of the National Provincial Bank Ltd issued in the 1930s. The fronts were relatively plain, but the beautifully engraved and coloured reverse sides more than compensated

The original logo of the American Express Company

A copy of the world's earliest surviving traveller's cheque, as issued by the American Express Company, and used to settle an hotel bill in Leipzig on 5 August 1891

An early twentieth-century traveller's cheque for $20 issued by the Fort Dearborn National Bank of Chicago. The bank issued other denominations of $10, $50 and $100, all carrying the finely engraved vignette. Such a long list of printed exchange rates was unusual and testifies to the stability of money markets at that era

Above: a bill dated 24 February 1819 at North Shields. Robert Spence, who signs the bill (the 'drawer') was a partner in the North & South Shields Bank (founded 1 Jan. 1819) . The bill instructs Frys & Chapman, the bank's London agents, to pay forty days after date the sum of £80 to the Receiver General of Post Office Revenue. Thus payment was due on 8 April, the date written at the top left. The bill also states 'value received of Thomas Oyston', which means Spence acknowledges receipt of goods or services worth £80 from Oyston, who was no doubt a local Post Office official. Notice that the bill is dated '2nd Month', rather than February; both sets of bankers were Quakers who refused to use the accepted names of months with their pagan derivations

Below: a bill dated 18 August 1819 at Quebec. Here, Henry French, a local merchant, instructs Linskill & Chapman, merchants of North Shields, to pay shipowner William Bruce in London the sum of £209 4s 1d for the use of the ship the *Three Brothers*. The difference from the above bill is that payment is to be made thirty days after sight, not date, so the voyage time has also to be added. Three copies of this bill would have been sent, but payment could have been made against any one. This is the second bill of the set. The cross-writing notes that on 13 November, Frys & Chapman (as bankers) accepted the bill on Linskill & Chapman's behalf. The eventual maturity date was 16 December (as entered top left), allowing a customary three days' grace, even after the stated period of credit

A seven-day post bill, issued in London, for travellers' use in the British Isles. The vignette shows St James's Palace, a few hundred yards from Herries's bank

A circular note issued in Paris for travellers' use on the Continent. The vignette shows the Herries coat of arms. Note the elaborate writing at either side of each document, designed to discourage forgery. Both read 'Sr Rt HERRIES & Co' on one side; on the other, the words are 'Cir POST BILL' and 'BRANCHE A PARIS' respectively

The experiment was soon abandoned, at least for the time being. If it ever really left the ground is doubtful. One reason was, of course, the predicted opposition of the Bank of England and established bankers; another was the absence of profit margins likely to wean correspondents away from existing practices. What the tourist thought of post bills was probably never tested; how landowners received them was evidently disappointing. The scheme also suffered from the failure of an important and mysterious 'proposal made [to Herries] for converting the affair . . . into a concern of Government: But on consulting the crown Lawyers this was found to be liable to objections, and to be exposed to much opposition in Parliament, and there the matter rests'.[19] This would seem to have been a move to have State taxes, and perhaps customs and excise dues, remitted to London by the new bills. The General Post Office was also interested, or consulted, because among its archives is a list of certain post towns in England and Wales where Herries had *not* succeeded in establishing correspondents.[20]

With these setbacks Herries temporarily abandoned the idea of his post bills having a secondary commercial application, and the scheme entered its second phase. He now concentrated on a more comprehensive service in post bills for foreign visitors who were crossing the Channel in increasing numbers. Much of the hard work in the pilot scheme was therefore wasted: 'the other papers on this business in your possession', Herries told his contacts, 'you will be pleased to put into the fire, lest they should perplex or mislead your clerks, as the present alterations render them quite useless'.[21] In January 1785, with a new determination, he circulated all his correspondents. This was partly, he explained, for information, in case a post bill somehow got presented by a tourist in mistake for a circular note; and partly to reassure them that no plans were afoot to change the system abroad.[22] But what he really wanted was a direct entry to foreigners' business via the intercession of their bankers. He saw the new service as offering a means to remit money into England from abroad, perhaps to sustain the long-term itinerary of a relation or friend, at a time when the rate of exchange was much against Europe. A paragraph explaining that Herries would exchange circular notes for post bills in London was appended to every letter of order on the foreign circuit.[23]

The earliest extant list of British and Irish towns where Herries succeeded in finding correspondents for his post bills, and the names of the twenty-six bankers or merchants there, dates from 2 February 1790.[24] It is reproduced on p. 89. The list is valuable as a glimpse of regional

COVER

For the Circular Poſt Bills of Sir ROBERT HERRIES *and Co. Bankers in* London, *which among other of the principal places (as well as at many of the Poſt Offices) in* Great Britain *and* Ireland, *may be chequed and verified at the following, ranged in alphabetical order, and oppoſite to theſe the names of the appointed Correſpondents who will honour thoſe Bills according to their tenor, in caſe the holders ſhould not, when ſo chequed, have paſſed them in payment to others wanting perhaps to remit to ſome of thoſe places, or to* London, *where, at all events, payment may be demanded.*

Aberdeen, ...	*Meſſrs.* Brebner and Co.	Lancaſter, ...	*Meſſrs.* A. and J. Rawlinſon.
Air, ...	—— Hunters and Co.	Leeds, ...	——
Banbury, ...,..	—— Thomas and Timothy Cobb.	Leiceſter, ...	—— Wm. and Edwd. Hodges.
Bath, ...	—— Robt. Clement.	Limerick, ...	—— Philip Roche John.
Berwick on Tweed,	—— Anthony Forſter.	Lincoln, ...	—— Robert Laurie.
Birmingham, ...	——	Liverpool, ...	—— Richard and Matthieſſen.
Brighthelmſtone, .	—— Harry Attree.	Londonderry, ...	—— John Coningham, Ferry-quay.
Briſtol, ...	—— Evan Baillie.	Lynn Regis, ...	—— Gurneys, Birkbeck, and Co.
Cambridge, ...	—— Mortlake and Francis.	Mancheſter, ...	—— Dinwiddie, Kennedy, and Co.
Carliſle, ...	—— Alexander Wilſon.	Margate, ...	—— F. Cobb and Son.
Cheltenham, ...	—— Bedwells.	Newcaſtle on Tyne,	—— Walter Hall and Co.
Cheſter, ...	—— W. H. Folliott.	Newmarket, ...	—— James Weatherby.
Cork, ...	—— Ferguſſon and Collow.	Norwich, ...	—— R. B. and J. Gurney.
Cowes, ...	—— James Mackenzie and Co.	Nottingham.	—— Davidſon and Hawkſley.
Dartmouth, ...	—— Arthur Holdſworth and Co.	Oxford, ...	—— Edward Lock and Son.
Dover, ...	—— Latham, Rice and Co.	Plymouth, ...	—— David Jardine, jun.
Dublin, ...	—— Robert Black and Co.	Poole, ...	—— Joſeph Garland and Co.
Dumfries, ...	—— Wm. Lawſon.	Portſmouth, ...	—— Andrew Lindegren.
Edinburgh, ...	—— Sir Wm. Forbes, J. Hunter, & Co.	Ramſgate, ...	—— Nathaniel Auſtin.
Exeter, ...	—— Barings, Short, and Cole.	Reading, ...	—— John Deane.
Falmouth, ...	—— Geo. C. Fox and Sons.	Saliſbury, ...	—— Dan. and Tho. Dyke.
Galway, ...	—— Pierce Joyce.	Sheffield, ...	—— Ashforth, Ellis and Co.
Glaſgow, ...	—— John Dunlop and Co.	Shrewſbury, ...	—— John Scott.
Glouceſter, ...	—— Turner and Jeynes.	Southampton, ...	—— Seward and Pipon.
Guernſey, ...	—— John Carey.	Topſham, ...	—— John Follett and Co.
Halifax, ...	—— Samuel and John Waterhouſe.	Tunbridge Wells, .	—— John Hutchinſon.
Harrowgate, ...	—— Jonathan Gilbertſon.	Waterford, ...	—— Simon Newport and Sons.
Haverford Weſt, .	—— Levy Phillips.	Whitehaven, ...	—— Dixon and Littledale.
Holyhead, ...	—— William Vickers, jun.	Yarmouth, ...	—— Manning, Meeke, Walker, & Harry.
Jerſey, ...	—— John Hue.	York, ...	—— William Teſſyman.

The utility of Circular Poſt Bills to Foreigners in tours of buſineſs or pleaſure in any of the three Kingdoms, and to others either on Law Circuits, at Elections, or at places of public reſort, is the more obvious from the riſks in carrying ſpecie, and the difficulty in aſcertaining the authenticity of public Banks or Bankers Notes, at a diſtance from their ſources; for without that the beſt paper in the hands of ſtrangers would be undervalued, in the ſame manner as gold itſelf would be, could it not be aſſayed at pleaſure. Thus the Circular Poſt Bills may, in that reſpect, claim a preference, while they neither can nor are meant to impede the circulation and eſtabliſhed currency of other paper ; the firſt for preventing loſs by robberies, &c. being only payable at any of the various places, on a preciſe day from preſentation, and the laſt on demand. Beſides the above Liſt, Travellers will occaſionally be furniſhed with recommendatory letters of order addreſſed to ſuch places as they may intend particularly to viſit ; and on the whole, the inſtitution of this branch will furniſh the means of facilitating the remittance of money to or from the capital, as well as from place to place in Great Britain *and* Ireland, *but not in Foreign Parts, where the Circular Notes of the ſame Houſe anſwer the like purpoſes.*

The traveller in Britain received a 'Cover' like the one issued to the traveller abroad. By this date, which could be around the turn of the eighteenth century, there were more than twice as many outlets, all over the British Isles, as there had been ten years earlier. Yet the post bill scheme was already doomed to failure

banking at a time when local directories, if they existed at all, were unreliable, and when a grey area existed between banking and the many callings from which the profession was coalescing. The functions of country banking evolved from the activities of men who built up reserves of money, or handled other people's, and were therefore able to use and loan those deposits to their own benefit. It was quite possible for a remitter of money himself to become a banker, as easily as could a brewer, draper or ironmaster, occupations more typically associated with the profession's rise.

Letter of Order.

London, the 2ᵈ Feb'y 1790

GENTLEMEN,

THIS Letter, which I deliver along with some of my Circular Post Bills to The Honble

will be presented at any of your respective places of residence, where he may have occasion to demand payment of any of them. You will be pleased to comply therewith, agreeable to my general instructions, and to give back the letter to him as it is intended to remain in his possession until the whole be paid.

You will observe by those instructions, that for the safety of the possessor, as well as to comply with the established usage in all Post Bills, the payment must not be anticipated; and that in Scotland and Ireland, it must be made at the course of Exchange, at the or London time, without any charge whatever at any of the places of payment.

I beg leave to recommend this Gentleman to your civilities, and to assure you, that I am truly

SIRS,

Your most obedient, humble servant

Places of Payment.	Payable by Messieurs.
Air	Hunters &Cº
Bath	Robᵗ Clement
Birmingham	Bery & Rob Blyth
Brighthelmstone	Harry Attree
Bristol	Evan Baillie
Cork	Ferguson & Hollow
	Cowes

In the same way as he issued notes for the English traveller abroad, Herries also issued them, known as circular post bills, for the foreigner (as well as the English person) who wished to travel in Britain. It is not clear when this practice began, but as there are only twenty-six places in this letter of order of 1790 (first page only reproduced), the scheme was still formative

Many firms prepared to act as correspondents for Herries in 1790 were actually mercantile houses, and some names (like Jardine at Plymouth and Cobb at Margate) were later to become famous in their own distinct fields of commerce and banking once the boundaries between those activities had crystallized. Clearly it was not easy to find correspondents, and firms entered for Birmingham, Leeds and Manchester had soon to be deleted. (Another list of correspondents, dated 10 March 1790, omits Birmingham and Leeds altogether, while Manchester has a new representation, by Messrs Dinwiddie, Kennedy & Co.)[25] It is noticeable that Herries had no agencies in Wales, but was represented in Scotland at Ayr, Dumfries, Edinburgh – by Forbes and Hunter, of course – and at Glasgow; he had contacts in Ireland at Cork, Dublin, Limerick, Londonderry and Waterford. If Guernsey is also excluded from the reckoning, the number of towns and cities actually in England where post bills could be presented is reduced to seventeen.

These were hardly enough outlets to support the inveterate traveller, especially as the choice of places reflected more the topographical accident of Herries's existing trading connections, than tourist routes. True, watering places were represented, like Bath, Brighton (given its original spelling of Brighthelmstone), and Harrogate. But the omission of Oxford, Cambridge and York, and of large towns like Leicester and Nottingham, was very unfortunate. Also, there was a lack of strategic agencies on the main posting routes. There was no correspondent at Dover or Canterbury for cross-Channel arrivals, no one at Salisbury or Exeter for the tourist going west, and no one at any stage of the Great North Road for the visitor to Scotland. As for Tyneside, there were no correspondents closer to Newcastle than Harrogate and Edinburgh.

And so the second phase of the post bill initiative ended as disastrously as the first. Perhaps this was the time to admit defeat, but Herries decided to have a last attempt. He needed to achieve two targets: the agency base had to be extended and the tourist market reinforced by a return to some wider commercial involvement. To achieve the first end, it was necessary to reintegrate the issuing of post bills into the firm of Sir Robert Herries & Co., rather than having it as a personal enterprise of its principal. This added a certain solidity to the undertaking as the firm became better known, and paved the way for Herries's associates to make a greater contribution to the scheme by introducing their own contacts.[26]

The result was very successful, at least on paper. The next surviving list of correspondents (p. 88) is nearly twice as long, at sixty, and the preamble claims that the towns in which they were located were 'among other . . .

principal places' where the scheme operated.[27] Birmingham and Leeds were obviously still troublesome but Wales was at last included, with agencies at Haverfordwest and Holyhead, while the service in Scotland and Ireland was enhanced by the addition of Aberdeen and Galway. The borders were strengthened by representation at Berwick, Newcastle and Carlisle, and most of the earlier anomalous gaps were filled expressly, or by implication. That last point connects to mention above of 'other principal places', and introduces the new commercial initiative which Herries was proposing. His target this time was the Post Office which already had his proposals under scrutiny.

In the 1790s the British postal service was far from being the integrated and State-run monopoly which it is today. The Postmaster-General and his staff exercised some central coordination from London but their main concern was for the six main roads, of very different lengths, radiating like spokes from the hub of London. The management of by- and cross-road letters had been farmed from 1719, for more than forty years, by Ralph Allen, the Bath philanthropist. When Allen died the administration of this business was moved from Bath to London as a separate branch of the General Post Office. But the postal sevice generally was still a horse-post and it took another luminary of Bath, John Palmer (1742–1818), to argue for the introduction of mail coaches. This was achieved in 1784, in the teeth of opposition from the Post Office itself, by the support of William Pitt.[28]

Travellers, both native and foreign, now used the mail coaches as a medium of travel, and the postmasters in larger towns as receivers of letters on their behalf. If Herries's interest in these postmasters began in the context of travel, it was the commercial possibilities of the postal service which added additional spice to his plan. Postmasters were salaried by the General Post Office, to whom they took an oath of allegiance and gave a bond for good conduct. They were usually innkeepers, and owners of fast coaches, who contracted for the service from one place to another. There were around five hundred of them when Herries showed his interest, contributing in large part to the Post Office's net profit of nearly a third of a million pounds a year.

Many postmasters, Herries claimed, would cash a seven-day post bill for a traveller collecting his mail in order to reuse the same bill, after endorsement, for remitting their takings to the General Post Ofice in London. Indeed, so would other people use them, he reckoned, who needed to send money to London or to any other town mentioned in the traveller's letter of order. Even those on Law Circuits, or out

Mail-coach routes, such an integral part of Herries's plans for a British equivalent of the circular note, improved quickly with the widespread establishment of turnpike roads in the second half of the eighteenth century. This map shows the system at its most developed state, in the decade before the railways began to menace its monopoly

electioneering, came within the trawl of Herries's latest casting, if we are to believe the prospectus.[29] But the postmasters were the real target. Herries consulted Palmer, who had been elevated to the appointment of Surveyor and Comptroller General of the Mails in 1786, as to the possibility of postmasters remitting by his seven-day post bills as a matter of course. As well as his salary, Palmer was to be paid $2\frac{1}{2}$ per cent of any net increase in revenues arising from his own innovations. He was therefore not likely to be uncooperative towards any scheme which

The York Royal Mail coach changing horses at a country stage, *c.* 1820

promised to increase his remuneration, nor was he the kind of man to be unsympathetic towards a fellow entrepreneur. Palmer, therefore, saw no difficulty with the scheme, but it was really a matter for the postmasters and their individual preferences for the means of quarterly remittance.[30]

Most postmasters contrived to send cash or good bills, not exceeding twenty-one days. Later, the incidence of remittance was made monthly, and even fortnightly if local revenue over fourteen days exceeded £70, as the Post Office tried to prevent postmasters making interim use of the money.[31] If they utilized Herries's post bills, thus sending him their proceeds in the first instance, he offered to pay them commission at the rate of ¼ per cent per month on the difference from their normal accounting date.[32] Unfortunately for Herries, Palmer was not long in his post. Irreconcilable disputes with the Postmaster General led to his suspension early in 1792 and dismissal soon after.

As if the loss of this influential contact was not damage enough, the tourist market was seriously undermined by the French Wars, and so both legs of the new proposition collapsed. The winding up of Herries's scheme is not recorded; indeed, it must be doubtful if it was ever so far in implementation as to need it. From the earliest stage the strategy confused tourist and commercial objectives, therefore lacking credibility to either camp. In a sense the post bill scheme was the antithesis of that for the circular note, the very instrument which had inspired its use: Herries had introduced the latter for travellers exactly because the alternatives for credit smacked too much of business and commerce. It was therefore a mistake to revert to a shared platform, particularly when other post bills already existed, notably those of the Bank of England, with whose pedigree and authority Herries could never hope to compete.

The last twitch of the dying system occurred neither on the Continent, nor in Britain itself, but in the British West Indies. The details lie in an undated 'Explanatory Cover for the West India Exchange Notes', which can be dated to around 1795.[33] It was as if the head of steam created by Herries, blocked in other outlets, was issuing through a safety valve at the far end of the boiler. Like all such issues, it made a spectacular exit and then evaporated into nothing. The idea was as follows: as the islands had no paper currency, and as specie was risky and expensive to send, and often debased on arrival, Herries thought that an instrument deriving both from circular notes and post bills would be of national, military, and commercial benefit. The State would gain by stamp duty, the army and navy would have an alternative to ready money for wages, payments and remittances, and traders would have an inter-island currency, useless to an enemy if it were captured. In Herries's words, this was to become 'a kind of Paper Currency in aid of Coin'. The dangers, however, were so real that no relaxation of the term of seven days from sight could be contemplated, and maybe for this reason, more than any other, the idea was abortive. As this proposal was not, in any event, motivated by concern for the tourist or traveller, we too can afford to abandon it.

Within Britain, meanwhile, the pastime of tourism was gaining momentum, with little regard for the privations of war. Indeed, the inability to travel abroad was itself a spur to make inland journeys, while the growing number of spas and watering places gave travelling for some people a new sense of purpose. Thus health and social acceptability joined curiosity and self-instruction as motives to set the English in movement in their own country in the early nineteenth century. That such movement became materially easier to undertake in terms of money supply, was itself a further incentive. This was due to improvements in the private banking system rather than to any contribution by Government to the amelioration of specie. For much of the eighteenth century the good standard of money introduced by a recoinage of 1696 had been squandered, with gold, silver and copper coins being clipped and worn to well below their nominal weight. In 1774 all light guineas were replaced by new and 'heavy' ones, but when the Bank of England, in 1797, was forced to suspend payment in gold for its banknotes, national coinage was rapidly in a critical condition. The bank even issued dollars, made from Spanish pieces of eight held as bullion, and tokens of 3s and 1s 6d, until political stability and technological advances combined to produce a satisfactory coinage from 1817.

Even from this date, however, it was still necessary to solve the problem of money supply once the traveller's initial full purse had been emptied. Correspondent relationships between bankers, such as have been discussed already in terms of Herries's post bills, made this much easier. In the eighteenth century banking in Britain developed along two lines: in London were the goldsmith-bankers and in the provinces were entrepreneurs who turned to banking to supplement or supersede some other business. The importance for country banks to have contacts with London has already been demonstrated, so agency arrangements were quickly established. The usefulness of this system to the tourist grew exactly in proportion to its spread. In around 1750, for instance, there were some twenty private banks in London but only about a dozen in the provinces, at least in England. By 1785, or roughly when Herries was experimenting with inland post bills, the ratio was beginning to change. The number of London banks had crept over fifty, but there were more than twice as many in the provinces. In 1800 there were nearly 70 London banks with another 370 recorded in the country at large. In another five years the ratio was 70 to 438; by 1810 it was 83 to 654 (or 783, depending on one's source). The volatile state of the national economy accounted for many failures but the number of country banks held at around 600 until the advent of English joint-stock banking in 1826.[34]

For a Londoner, or for a foreign tourist arriving in London, it was possible to call at a bank and lodge specie (unless, of course, an account was already held there) against a supply of paper credit payable at the bank's country agencies. It follows from the figures above that one London bank could have several agency arrangements, and the older firms had far more than their mathematical share: Glyn, Mills & Co., for example, established in the City in 1753, created eighty-two country agencies before 1820.[35] Even without such a comprehensive passport to the provinces, the traveller was in a good position. If he wished to visit a particular town, he had only to establish, from directories, the name of the local banking firm and contact its London agent(s). Similarly, the countryman coming up to London could call at his local bank for an arrangement in the other direction. Once the traveller reached his provincial town, he would often find that his bank had branches elsewhere, or agencies in the sense of local traders or firms who would tout for business and honour its paper. This widened to a modest extent the traveller's circle of movement, in terms of his money supply, and in practice the paper of most well-established local banks was accepted by other bankers who operated in overlapping or adjacent areas.

There were various types of paper for the traveller to take. At the one extreme were still bills of exchange, but the relatively long maturity dates, when mail coaches travelling on turnpiked roads were reducing journey times, made these an increasingly obsolete form of provision. Post bills, payable a few days after date or sight, were safe and sufficient, and it was not now too incautious, with better security on main roads, to take bills payable on demand – that is to say, cheques. Drawn on the traveller's London bank, these could be made payable to bearer or to order at any of its country agencies or vice versa.

Another form of paper, payable on demand, was of course the banknote. These would be Bank of England notes if issued in London, but local notes if issued in the provinces. According to the stature of the bank of issue, such notes attracted in the bearer varying degrees of confidence as to his ability to redeem them for specie at face value. When confidence was low, and people tried to cash-in their notes at the same time (a situation known as a 'run'), many bankers found themselves over-exposed, and failed.[36] In such cases note-holders might receive a modest dividend on their paper when bankruptcy had run its course, but often such failure could be ruinous for customer and banker alike. But of course banknotes were used mainly not as an instrument for acquiring cash, but as cash itself, and therefore they were the most flexible provision in the traveller's wallet.

Although many people were brave enough to carry wads of banknotes on long journeys within Britain, especially on the advent of steam locomotion, it was common practice until the mid-nineteenth century to cut each note in two, carry one half, and send the other separately to the destination address. This practice had been invariable in the eighteenth century. As the serial number of a note was recorded at either end, there was usually no difficulty in matching halves, and bankers grew tolerant to the submission of mutilated paper. Against an indemnity, it was even possible to encash only one half, if there were a plausible story for the loss of the other.[37]

The practice of cutting notes owes much to the General Post Office, which issued printed notices of encouragement, while special adhesive labels were available to reunite the halves on arrival.[38] Meanwhile, the Post Office itself ran a money order office from 1792 (introduced on the private initiative of Clerks of the Road) for the dispatch of sums not exceeding £5. This facility, with a small charge to sender and receiver, involved a system of money orders payable at sight by the deputy postmaster at the place of destination. Despite high usage, money orders became an official Post Office service only in 1838.[39] They were suitable for people on a predetermined itinerary, but most travellers would have found bank paper more useful; so the real value of the Post Office was as a means to convey cheques and maybe banknotes from family, or a friend, at base to the traveller at a *poste restante* address. Such payments were sent in the ordinary letter post against official advice but at very low risk.

As far as country bankers were concerned, tourists, foreign or otherwise, were no more than fair game in the pursuit of business. If a dimension of hospitality is sought such as has been seen for the British abroad, then it was arranged or offered among personal contacts, rather than as an extension of the business of money supply. The routine entertainment of foreigners played not the least part in the social diary of the provincial banker. The situation was not quite the same in London, where many of the long-established bankers were such travellers themselves, or such patrons of the fine arts, or were so well connected socially, that some hospitality for the best class of foreigner would have been offered as a matter of course.

There is, curious to relate, at least one recorded instance of a prospective Grand Tourist enjoying the perks of European banking before she had even left the mainland. The lady in question, Mrs Trench, was travelling in 1799 via Great Yarmouth, where there were fears for her comfort owing to possible delays in the departure of her ship. When these fears were realized, Mrs Trench was duly grateful for the kind attentions of Mr Hudson Gurney, a local banker, to whom she had 'a letter of Mr Sanford's; who without knowing . . . him, recommended me to his care, feeling wretched at the idea of my being unprotected in the first stage of my journey'.[40]

The foreign traveller in Britain found no expatriate bankers, such as his British counterpart found abroad; none, that is, until the Frankfurt-born Nathan Rothschild settled in London in 1805, at the same time as his brothers James and Solomon settled in Paris and Vienna. It appears that the stance of Nathan towards his many German customers reflected the businesslike position which the Rothschilds had established on the Continent. Their bank having being excluded, as we have noticed, from the social relationships which characterized the business of their Christian colleagues, there was no reason for attitudes to change simply because traffic was established in the other direction.

The best description of Rothschild, from a tourist's pen, comes from Prince Pückler-Muskau, visiting London in 1826. The first point which struck him was the contrast between the status of the 'real lion' of the City of London, and his 'insignificant location' in St Swithin's Lane. He then reported that Rothschild did not stand on ceremony. 'When I handed him my letter of credit, he remarked ironically that we rich people were fortunate in being able to travel about and amuse ourselves; while on him, poor man, there rested the cares of the world, and, he went on, bitterly bewailing his lot, no poor devil came to England without wanting something from him.' Rothschild told him that, the day before, a Russian had begged him for money and 'the Germans here don't give me a moment's peace'.[41] In assessing this attitude, it must also be taken into account that Rothschild was not, properly speaking, a banker, but a merchant banker. The distinction may seem pedantic but is of real importance. It is in vain that names like Rothschild and Baring are sought in early lists of London bankers – that is to say, among members of the London clearing house. Their customers were truly international, and it was logical, if such bankers held accounts of foreign governments, that representatives and dignitaries from those countries should make use of their services when visiting Britain.

By the middle of the nineteenth century the tourist found yet another level of banking to compete for his business. He could now use joint-stock banking companies to even more advantage than earlier alternatives. The reasons for the introduction of joint-stock banking in England, by Acts of 1826 and 1833, need not be discussed here, but it should be realized that there was a basic difference between a banking firm (i.e. a private bank) and a banking company. The former was a partnership and restrictive legislation engineered by the Bank of England limited the number of principals to six.[42] This was an effective check to growth, not least territorially, and few private banks had more than half a dozen branches, while many had none at all.

For joint-stock companies, however, with several hundred shareholders or 'proprietors', branch banking was central to the strategy. There existed the capital base and organization to initiate a network of outlets, and the business determination to support it. Within the first decade of Victoria's reign, it was possible to open an account with such a bank and have access to areas of Britain on a scale with which the private banks could not compete. The most notable example was the National Provincial Bank, established in 1833. By 1845 it had sixty branches and thirty-two sub-branches, ranging from Dover to Aberystwyth, and Plymouth to Darlington. That was quite exceptional, but at the same date the London & County Bank had thirty-six branches, and in Scotland, where joint-stock banking had much earlier beginnings, the Commercial Bank of Scotland had fifty-two offices north of the border, with the British Linen Company, and several other banks, not far behind.[43] Although a position was never reached in Britain, before the telephone and computer, where it was possible to call at a strange branch of one's own bank, armed only with a cheque book, and withdraw money as a matter of course, the prudent traveller was able to negotiate arrangements with branches in the areas he was visiting.

May it then be concluded that Europeans touring Britain from the mid-nineteenth century were without monetary worry? Alas, no. The root of the trouble lay in our aloofness from the Latin Monetary Union, established in 1865, which was mentioned in the last chapter. Although only France, Italy, Belgium and Switzerland were the founding members, Greece joined three years later and Holland and Germany were unofficial participants. So a French tourist, for example, carrying only 20 franc pieces, found that hoteliers over much of western Europe took them without question, and at par. When the Frenchman came to London, however, he found our money '*un embarras de toutes les minutes*'. Not only was French gold not accepted but neither were sous, which were exactly the same nominal value as pennies. The government claimed a discrepancy in bronze content, alleging that fishermen of Calais loaded their boats with French sous, sailed to Dover, and exchanged them for British pennies, thereby making a killing by the difference in intrinsic values.[44]

To Jules Degrégny, visiting London in 1888, the situation was quite clear: the English did not want contact with the Continent. In his view it was not in the interest of the aristocracy, who controlled the government, to promote better relations between their subjects and the free people, as he called them, of Europe. '*Ce sentiment, non moins que la crainte d'une invasion, entretient la résistance au projet de tunnel sous-marin,*' he concluded, the point of which is not lost on us today. Degrégny's advice was to buy enough English money in Paris or Calais to cover projected expenses in London, as to buy funds in London itself was to lose heavily on the exchange rate.[45]

As we leave Degrégny cursing the visual confusion between a florin and half-a-crown, it is worth pondering briefly whether the advance of one hundred years or so has really made any difference in the European conception of the attitude of the British towards the Europeans.

5
BEATING THE BORDER: SOME FRONTIER PROBLEMS AND THEIR PARTIAL SOLUTION

At various times in this narrative the impression has been given that money was some kind of passport to contentment; that the traveller's only practical concern abroad was the realization of his credit and the manipulation of his banker. But a literal kind of passport was a more immediate requirement and money played a significant role getting the traveller through the several annoyances of a border crossing. Sometimes money alone was not enough, and the banker himself could be called upon to effect a traveller's entry, or, more usually, his departure.

The 'annoyances' to be examined are passports, health control and customs, the great levellers of rank and privilege. They are, of course, connected, to some extent by historical evolution, invariably by location, and often by the identity of examining officials. Many countries connected passport and customs checks with control on the export of specie. It would be wrong, however, to consider the requirement for passports as confined to international boundaries, and it helps to understand the derivation of the second syllable as being from 'port', in the sense of a town gate, as well as from port meaning a harbour. This will be clearer if a little time is spent looking at the evolution of passports and their place in the study of travellers' money.

First, the modern concept of a passport as a standardized instrument of *laissez-passer*, applicable the world over, must be forgotten. But if it is borne in mind that certain foreign countries require the supplement of a visa then the particular and temporary usage for which passports were traditionally intended can be more readily understood. Another point is that passports have their origins in licences, or permits, of absence dating from Medieval and Tudor times; in other words they were essentially a permission to leave Britain rather than an authority to enter a foreign

state. In 1434 alone, nearly 2,500 such licences were issued by Henry VI
for pilgrimages to northern Spain.[1]

It soon became essential on the continent of Europe to carry an official
document requesting that the traveller pass freely, without let or
hindrance, and was entitled to the assistance and protection of
whomsoever it may concern. In practice, of course, the traveller saw less
of the rights and courtesies which his document demanded and more of
the harassment of officialdom. Several passports of this kind could be
required in the course of a single journey. Tourists had to report to the
governor's office at the port or frontier town, reveal their identity, and be
equipped with paper which would allow them to leave, by the appropriate
gate, to continue their journey or return home. These were expensive
procedures, involving fees to placate the military and service the
bureaucracy. At gates of subsequent fortified towns the routine was re-
enacted, to the exasperation of travellers like Hester Piozzi, in 1784:

> Few things upon a journey contribute to torment and disgust one
> more than the teasing enquiries at the door of every city, who one is,
> what one's name is? what one's rank in life or employment is; that so
> all may be written down and carried to the chief magistrate for his
> information, who immediately dispatches a proper person to examine
> whether you gave in a true report; . . . with twenty more inquisitive
> speeches, which to a subject of more liberal governments must
> necessarily appear impertinent as frivolous. . . .[2]

In fact, in comparison with experiences in earlier centuries, this was one of
the better times to travel. Tourists who had adequate letters of introduction,
and were careful or lucky in their choice of route, could get by with little
bother and a minimum of passports. Such relaxation of control was spoilt by
the French Revolution, as Arthur Young discovered. It was still possible for
him to reach North Italy from Nice without any passport at all, but in France
itself he made the mistake of deviating from a pre-arranged itinerary, precisely
on account of the troubles. Despite carrying letters to reputable men in many
provincial towns, he could not get a passport from a lawyer in Besançon
because he had no contacts there. In Young's eyes, this was revolutionary
nonsense: 'These passports are new things from new men, in new power'. His
anger was such that he published every alleged word of the dialogue with the
lawyer, a man dismissed by Young as '*un commis de bureau*' (an office boy). Had
he known a banker or merchant in Besançon he would have had less
difficulty, but in any event he could still move around.[3]

George Forster, at roughly the same time, was facing far worse problems in Asia, as 'no person, except by stealth, can enter or depart from Kashmire, without an order, marked with the seal of government'. Masquerading as a Turk, for reasons of personal security, Forster applied to the governor, by an intermediary, for a passport to leave. No, replied the governor: Turks are good soldiers; he can join our army instead. In horror Forster turned to the local banker who had cashed his draft from Jumbo. Can you get me a passport? Yes, said the banker, but immediately fell foul of the authorities on the question of a government loan. Forster was now desperate and recruited a Georgian of his acquaintance as another intermediary.[4]

This man was at last successful 'by an unremitted attendance of fifteen days, aided by a small bribe'. Ten miles out of Kashmir city Forster exchanged his passport for a new one at the River Jhelum. The tension relaxed; Forster felt a free man. He fell asleep 'pluming' himself on having outwitted the governor. The following night, however, while still on the border, he had his overcoat stolen and in it was the passport. You must apply all over again, said the frontier guard – words which might have finished a man of lesser calibre. But Forster knew an occasion for a bribe when he met one, and rupees did the trick. Three hundred yards later, however, four men raced up and arrested him as a state criminal, for return to the capital. Again Forster saw the cue for a substantial payout. Wholly on account of a passport, he left Kashmir a much poorer man than he had entered it.[5]

For entry into Britain the necessity of a passport was a by-product of the French Revolution, almost a retaliation for the indignities suffered by the British in France in 1792. With the situation there deteriorating fast, some two thousand Britons descended on Paris in August, using every kind of go-between – diplomat, friend, or banker – to get their passport to safety.[6] Within a few months Parliament in London passed *An Act for establishing regulations respecting aliens . . .*, part of which, from 10 January 1793, enforced visitors to Britain to register their names and ranks at the port of entry; no aliens were to depart inland without a passport from the local mayor, or the chief magistrate, or a justice of the peace, and all, save merchants, had to state their destination.[7] (These provisions were somewhat amended in 1798.) It comes as no surprise that, in Britain, the name of one's banker or merchant was not given or requested as a passport referee.

When the continent of Europe was reopened after 1815 it was impossible to go anywhere without much forethought and preparation for frontier controls. Never had the ability and inclination to travel been stronger, and never had the pettiness of restrictions been more exasperating. Passports were inspected at fortified towns, could be demanded at any time by the police (who were established earlier in many European countries than in Britain) and were usually required by innkeepers who had to submit names and nationalities of guests to local officialdom. A Briton embarking on the Grand Tour had to be clear as to his itinerary, selecting appropriate passports with one eye on the fast-changing political atlas, especially in the Low Countries and northern Italy.

If he were simply going to France he applied in London for a free passport from the French ambassador; or he could apply for one at major ports of entry with expense and greater formality. If his destination was Germany, life was more complex, depending on the route. Passports were needed from the French, Belgian or Dutch ambassadors, if any of these countries were visited on the way, but if he sailed direct to Hamburg he needed only a 5s passport from the consul to the Hanseatic towns.[8] An alternative was to buy a Foreign Office passport for a fee of two guineas and have it countersigned (the French term for this was *visé*, hence our word visa) by the ambassadors of every country to be visited – a procedure which could take several days. Representatives of foreign powers in London sometimes needed reassurance as to the respectability of applicants for passports, and in such cases London bankers gave a confidential opinion.[9]

Clearly, in this period the notion of a 'British passport' as simple evidence of the nationality of the holder does not enter the reckoning. It was sometimes advisable, and indeed unavoidable, for a Briton to travel under foreign protection. It could also be easier to acquire a passport abroad from a foreign source than a British one. When Charles Maclean left Hamburg for Paris in 1801 he was equipped with a Dutch passport as the British representative felt it politically wrong to grant him one. In Vienna he applied for a Spanish ambassador's passport to go to Cadiz.[10] In Paris, in 1814, Captain Barlow rejected a French passport because it cost 10 francs. But the British ambassador would only give him one with a certificate from Barlow's Parisian banker as to his nationality: his name was shared with a prominent family from America with which Britain was then at war.[11]

A British Foreign Office passport, acquired in London with appropriate visa at the outset of the journey, was the norm from around 1830. The cost rose to £2 7s 6d but fell sharply to 7s 6d in February 1851. This

We, James Howard, Earl of Malmesbury, Viscount Fitz-Harris, Baron Malmesbury, a Peer of the United Kingdom of Great Britain and Ireland, a Member of Her Britannic Majesty's Most Honourable Privy Council, Her Majesty's Principal Secretary of State for Foreign Affairs, &c., &c., &c.

Request and require, in the Name of Her Majesty, all those whom it may concern to allow Mr. Thomas Francis Cobb *(British Subject) accompanied by his family, travelling on the Continent,*

to pass freely without let or hindrance, and to afford him every assistance and protection of which he may stand in need.

Given at the Foreign Office, London, the 14th day of July 1852.

Signature of the Bearer

Foreign Office passport issued to Mr T.F. Cobb and family in 1852 for a European tour. Showing through at the top are endorsements of the Sardinian and Austrian legations in London, indicating that the itinerary was to include areas now part of the south of France and north Italy

made a dramatic difference to numbers issued: 1,178 in the calendar year before the reduction, and 7,304 in the year following.[12] Unfortunately, the mid-century traveller found cheapness at home was not matched abroad by relaxation of controls. The most vexatious country was Austria, whose occupation of northern Italy made its regulations applicable in areas where many tourists considered they had no right to be. Most diarists have anecdotes or personal recollections of Austrian passport control, as they deviated from their itinerary 'for this stupid form, from the most stupid of governments'[13] or returned a hundred miles for a neglected signature. Pent-up frustrations, like the following of M.F. Tupper, erupt on the printed page:

> Seven times within ten hours have I – a private English-gentleman traveller, with ladies in company, and all other circumstances of harmlessness and respectability, – been subjected to a most suspicious and vexatious vise of my passport. Seven times have [Austrian] military heroes watched me in and out of trains, in and out of cities; and once among the seven they kept me for three-quarters of an hour kicking my heels in an office while a clerk was cross-questioning and browbeating my worthy. . .[guide] Pierre.[14]

Even a minor breach of protocol could be an expensive mistake, as E. Wilkey discovered in Berlin. Intending to visit Austrian territory, he asked their ambassador to *viser* his existing passport. But it was a Hanseatic consular document, which was not acceptable. Wilkey had to obtain a new one from the English chargé d'affaires in Berlin and have it countersigned by the minister for foreign affairs, the police, and the ambassadors of Saxony and, finally, Austria. What he should have done, he learnt later, was have the English visa applied to his consular passport before it was submitted to the Austrians.[15]

Soon continental passport restrictions, not simply around Austrian territory, were exciting resentment among a much wider section of the travelling public. We can instance the following tirade by T.N. Talfourd, who was also a champion of Free Trade:

> Surely the system of passports is wholly unworthy of civilised, peaceful Europe in the nineteenth century! If any security could be attained by it against the admission of dangerous persons, or if any fees were really derived from it, some excuse might be found for its continuance . . . the entire suavity of temper which Mr Murray

A mid-nineteenth-century impression of a German official handling, with no great delicacy, the passport of a deferential traveller

recommends to all travellers, is in some danger of being broken. In truth, the whole is a vexatious farce – very foolish in the States, which profit by English gold – and very annoying to the travellers who are eager to scatter it.[16]

Restrictions were all the more irksome to travellers who had been further afield and found attitudes more relaxed. A 'rambler' from Sydney to Southampton received his first ever passport in South America in 1847, and 'a fine fidget' it made of him, as he entered Peru. For an exit passport, he drove from Lima to Callao where a long wait was rewarded by a handsome document with half a dozen elaborate signatures and two or three seals. There was also, to his consternation, a paragraph as to his personal appearance, composed hastily by the clerk at the interview. 'He put me down as having amongst other ornaments, red hair, blue eyes, an aquiline nose, and tall stature: not one of which things do I possess. . . .' If this was bureaucracy, however, it was nothing compared with the procedure at Havana, where exit passports were obtained only through agents, on the strength of certificates from the police, customs, and one's national consul that nothing was amiss. This document cost $10 in fees, on top of the $4 to land in the first place, and various customs fees. Our rambler was not impressed: 'A regular swindling place is Havannah, from one end to the other'.[17]

Another British traveller, J. Frith, had a curious incident with his Foreign Office passport in San Francisco in the early 1850s. He had received a cheque from New York and took it to a bank to be cashed. The cashier wanted proof of identity, preferably from some local person,

Havana, capital of Cuba, showing the Exchange. The city's strategic and commercial importance came from its harbour (the name Havana derives from the Spanish word for 'haven'), capable of taking a thousand ships at a time, but approached through the narrowest of fortified entrances

like a hotel-keeper. Frith thought no one locally knew him well enough, so he fetched his passport, countersigned for Italy and Germany. The cashier was quite excited. 'The sight of this servile relic of barbarous and feudal ages seemed to interest his curiosity, for he said, "Well, I never saw a document of this sort before, although I have read of them, and heard my countrymen who have been in Europe speak of them."' When amazement subsided, Frith got his money.[18]

To understand the North American insouciance for passports, one need only read Mark Twain's account of his excursion to Europe in 1867. His ship carried a 'Commissioner of the United States of America to Europe, Asia, and Africa', a title so awe-inspiring to Twain that he wondered why 'a dignitary of that tonnage' was not taken apart and carted over in sections, in several vessels, as a safety precaution.[19] This official seemed to make individual passports of less consequence. Only at Constantinople did the Americans worry, when they were warned about controls at Sebastopol, the next port of call.

'I had lost my passport', admitted Twain, 'and was travelling under my room-mate's, who stayed behind in Constantinople to await our return. To read the description of him in that passport and then look at me, any man could see that I was no more like him than I am like Hercules. So I went into the harbour of Sebastopol with fear and trembling – full of a vague, horrible apprehension that I was going to be found out and hanged. But all that time my true passport had been floating gallantly overhead – and behold it was only our flag. They never asked us for any other.'[20]

In Britain, by the turn of the nineteenth century, passport acquisition had returned to the domain of banking. It was normal for most bankers not only to support applications but to see them through in a time-scale we would now find bewildering. Customers were advised not to delay applying until the last moment as the Foreign Office required one day's notice before issuing a passport, except in very urgent cases. Branch bankers readily gave information and advice, and held stocks of passport application forms which, on completion, they transmitted to London head office for lodgement with the Foreign Office. This form was supported by a certificate of recommendation and identity, which introduced the applicant and vouched for his or her British nationality.[21] Bankers could still obtain passports for intending travellers until well into the 1950s.

Will you be away for long?

If you are a customer of Lloyds Bank, arrangements can be made for you to draw money at the Bank's branches or from agents throughout the British Isles.

When you are going abroad, the Manager of any branch can tell you the amount of money which may be taken and furnish you with a Letter of Credit, Travellers' Cheques and foreign money. Lloyds Bank will gladly give you guidance on questions arising out of exchange control and, if you wish, obtain your passport for you.

Let LLOYDS BANK

look after *your* interests

A Lloyds Bank travel advertisement for 1953, the last year in which the bank publicly offered to obtain passports for intending travellers

It has been seen that a passport to leave a country was every bit as important as a passport to enter, and one of the roots of this requirement lay in the dread of contagious diseases. In some countries a licence to depart depended on the possession of a bill of health, signifying the well-being of the traveller and sometimes the freedom from infection of the locality as a whole. If these could not be certified, then a journey could be indefinitely suspended. These requirements are found at places as far apart as Smyrna and Batavia until the middle of the nineteenth century. Such fears and phobias were as old as travel itself, and apparently older than written certificates. When Fynes Moryson arrived at Nancy from Poland in 1594 he had to swear at the town gate that Poland was free of the plague.[22] Travellers to north Italy in the seventeenth century found the requirement for bills of health began at Lyons, and they were quite essential for entering Venice. Indeed in all Venetian possessions, such as

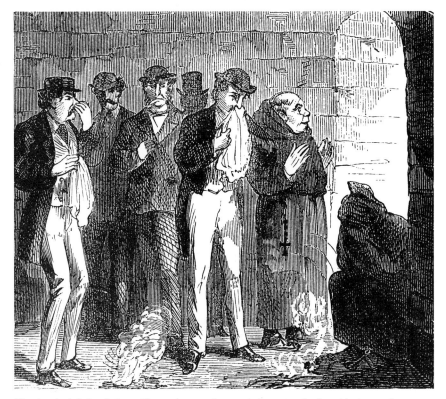

The dread of cholera led to widespread quarantine regulations, even in the mid-nineteenth century, and sometimes to compulsory five-minute fumigation for tourists. Mark Twain's sketch of the event at Bellagio in north Italy is charming enough, but it was a nasty experience: like 'the Black Hole of Calcutta on a small scale . . . a smoke that smelt of all the dead things of earth, of all the putrefaction and corruption imaginable'

Crete, the same procedures were adopted; visitors entered a so-called lazaretto where they were questioned and documentation was examined. If all was not well, they were required to '*far' la Quarantana*', that is spend forty days in isolation, from where comes the modern word quarantine.[23]

The Venetian system owed its stringency to trade with Constantinople, where plague was endemic. Travellers who landed at that city by sea had their luggage thrown into horse-hair bags, thought to be infection proof, and were given sticks to keep people and loose dogs at a distance. Franks (that is, Western Europeans) were particularly nervous. The vicar of Godalming saw a lady weakened by seasickness faint on the hill from Galata to Pera: she was left to her own devices. When positive symptoms appeared, patients were deserted by their families and their doctors. Native Turks, on the other hand, were said to be scornful of the disease, 'vying with each other for the honor of bearing a plague corpse a few paces on its road to the grave, and preserving or selling the clothes of the deceased'.[24]

The perceived fear from plague was more in terms of contagion than airborne infection, and this made money-changing very difficult, especially as metal was judged a potent 'conductor' of disease. The acceptable solution in Turkey, until the mid-nineteenth century, was the passage of coins through water. A banker paying out to a traveller placed the money on a flat, triangular board, with a rim. At one angle the rim was missing so that the money could drop into a vase of water. The contents of the vase were then deemed non-contagious and poured back carefully on the tray, so that the money stayed in position. Only then was it handled by the customer.[25]

Paper, whether money, passport, or bill of health, was obviously not amenable to the water treatment and gave rise to a pantomime of precautions, usually involving tongs. When the Revd Mr Walsh reached Bucharest one evening in 1829, his arrival had been anticipated by the plague. He went through a process of fumigation at the Austrian consulate, to where he had letters of introduction, and then went in search of the merchant on whom he had a letter of credit. The money was handed over without ceremony as Mr Walsh, the recipient, was unruffled by risk of contagion. The difficulty was over the receipt as the clerk was not equally confident about Mr Walsh. He was 'greatly embarrassed how he should take it . . . without touching it. He at length found an iron spoon in the room, and taking out a piece of oil-cloth, he shovelled the paper into the folds of it; then holding it at arm's length, and carefully turning it, so that it should not be between him and the wind, he hastily departed'. With all due respect for the horrors of the plague, Walsh found it all 'exquisitely ridiculous'.[26]

When the incidence of bubonic plague diminished, precautions were kept alive by the fear of cholera. As the nineteenth century progressed, quarantine arrangements, particularly around the Mediterranean shores, seemed to intensify. Again Italy was in the vanguard of prevention. Now travellers from the south of France into the Riviera di Genoa could be met at Nice by Sardinian soldiers, carrying rifle and tongs. Even certificates of quarantine at Marseilles were of no avail and seven days in a lazaretto at Villa Franca befell many latter-day Grand Tourists.[27] We can well imagine what Smollett would have said about that, or Mrs Piozzi.

Some stories arising from nineteenth-century quarantine requirements border on farce. Emma Roberts recalled how she, and her friend 'Miss E.', on their journey from England to Bombay in 1839, stopped over at Malta. With political tension rising in the Near East, they decided to leave Malta quickly by the mail steamer bound for Alexandria. But the ship was offshore in quarantine. The Maltese authorities took them out in a launch, towing a small boat. When they reached the steamer the officials put the ladies and their luggage in the same small boat and kept well away. There was no help from the steamer and had any of the land officials touched it they would have spent the next eighteen days in quarantine. With no assistance from either side, Miss E. had to hook her parasol on to the anchor line to prevent them drifting away.[28]

Britain was not exempt from quarantine arrangements but was slow to introduce them. For some years London-bound cargo boats from the Mediterranean lay up in Standgate Creek in the River Medway and could, if necessary, discharge their cargoes into four old warships equipped as lazarettos.[29] But regulations were progressively relaxed and Parliament, in 1844, resolved to encourage further sensible revisions in Britain and abroad.[30] With such encouragement unheeded on the Continent, travellers found ways of getting round the restrictions. Mark Twain, with others of his party, pre-empted quarantine at Naples by going ashore at Civita Vecchia, thence to Rome, and then on by train. There were no restrictions into Naples by land and Twain pulled faces from the shoreline at fellow passengers roasting for ten days in Naples Bay.[31]

That was, arguably, a legitimate infringement of the health laws but Twain's escapades soon after at Piraeus were definitely illegal. The ship arrived in the harbour, to be ordered out again immediately; the choice was between sailing on, and eleven days' quarantine. The captain decided to head for Constantinople but needed twelve hours, or an overnight stay,

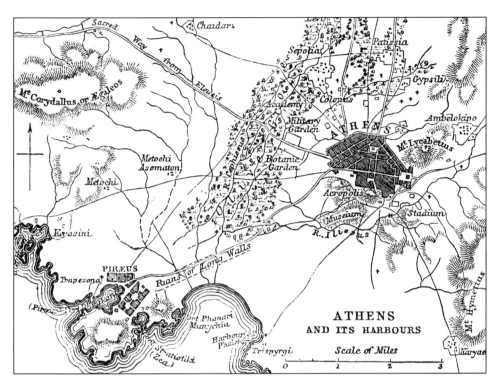

The still-country route from Piraeus to the Acropolis, at the time Mark Twain made his illegal excursion. The port of Piraeus only became really established in 1834. Earlier, Queen Caroline's entourage noted that the Turkish customs officer there was 'a model of stupid patience: whole months elapse without . . . the arrival of a single vessel'

to take on supplies. The forbidden fruit of the Acropolis was too much for some to behold. All too aware of the penalties, Twain and three companions 'stole softly ashore in a small boat', just before midnight. It was almost a disaster from the beginning, as people still aboard could follow their progress by the barking of loose dogs. They reached their goal but had the misfortune to steal grapes on the way back and spent some time under an armed escort of vineyard owners. When they reached the beach at dawn, after thirteen miles, encircled by the usual pack of stray dogs, a police boat was just offshore looking specifically for quarantine breakers. They managed to send it the wrong way, while their own small boat arrived for a rapid and inglorious rescue.[32]

Such derring-do is a little removed from the theme of travellers' money, but quarantine did have very definite financial implications. Although a lazaretto could be a miserable hole, especially on the border between Moldavia and Russia,[33] the principle was not always detrimental to commerce. In many harbours, such as Marseilles, Genoa and Leghorn, ships could discharge directly into lazarettos and continue on their way, the goods being 'purified' before release. Such systems encouraged the rise of an entrepôt, where the enforced presence of merchants, diplomats and bankers added an element of stability. The classic example is, ironically, Beirut which (as Beyroot) developed fast in the nineteenth century as the port and quarantine for Syria. Bankers and money-changers followed and a British visitor, even by the 1830s, found that 'consuls representing the principal European powers have raised their flags here, and everything indicates an increase of wealth and importance'. The quarantine period for vessels from Constantinople and Smyrna was a hot eleven days, after which it was a relief for crews to come ashore and spend their money.[34]

It is now appropriate to consider customs, the last of the frontier impediments to harass the undeserving traveller. For evidence of their nuisance value, the historian is thoroughly spoilt for choice; catalogues of delay, indignity and impertinence hijack the traveller's pen. While passports, bills of health and quarantine could sometimes be avoided, the protectionist instinct of trading countries made frontier checks inevitable. Although there were legitimate ways in which the customs service impinged upon travellers' money and travellers' bankers, the venality of officials was such that far more cash was spent in oiling the frontier wicket-gate than in government dues. In fact the travel journal in which a customs official does not accept tips to spare himself the trouble of a search is very much the exception.

Sometimes travellers were spared the embarrassment of making the offer and risking indignation. When Dr Maclean was embarking at Bordeaux in 1803 he was approached by a smart customs officer, green-uniformed and very polite, with the words: 'I hope you will think of me, Sir; I have allowed your baggage to pass without examination'.[35] The award for best anecdote, however, must be given to Mrs van Tets, passing into France from her native Holland in 1819. At the last of several lines of customs posts, the officer said: 'You have probably nothing against the laws of the kingdom, but if you will let me drink your health, I dare not accept anything, but be so kind as to give it to this child who will pass it on to me'.[36]

The worst experiences for travellers came when money was inappropriate, or refused, or when officials were over-protective of the local economy. Mrs Piozzi had characteristically strong views: 'But these Customhouse officers!', she ranted, struggling through north Italy in 1784, 'these *rats de cave*, as the French comically call them, will not let a

At Civita Vecchia, the port for Rome, Mark Twain had his baggage searched by Customs officers who confiscated one of his jokes as an 'incendiary document'. Twain was philosophical: 'I suppose it will be sent up and filed away among the criminal archives of Rome, and will always be regarded as a mysterious infernal machine which would have blown up like a mine and scattered the good Pope all around, but for a miraculous providential interference'.

ribbon pass. Such is the restless jealousy of little states, and such their unremitted attention to keep the goods made in one place out of the gates of another'.[37] It was a common enough policy. Piedmontese border officials were fanatical about keeping Swiss watches out of France and the Prussians showed 'saucy arrogance' in keeping '*Englische waaren*' out of their country.[38]

The Prussians also exacted \$20 (£3) from everyone crossing their border out of Holstein and Mecklenburg. To many this was a racket, although a middle-class Grand Tourist, like E. Spencer, felt it a good way to keep out the riff-raff. 'If this admirable precaution were in force in England', he suggested, 'we should not be inundated with German broom-girls, Italian vagabonds, and pennyless strollers. . . .'[39] Less pleased with officious behaviour was Charles Tennant, crossing into Germany from the Low Countries in 1821, by an unfrequented customs post. Forgetting the simple formality of removing his hat, he was subjected to a rare catalogue of incivilities and paid duty on a blunderbuss at six times the normal tariff.[40]

Women were often outraged at their own treatment, particularly as the nineteenth century progressed. Mrs Mary Roget arrived at Le Havre in 1830 to be examined by a woman customs officer: 'I might have been spared the annoyance of having her hand inserted underneath my stays,' was her acid reminiscence.[41] The American Catherine Sedgwick heard dreadful tales of the Austrians in Lombardy: 'A Milanese lady . . . told me they had given up going to it [i.e. the border] on account of the indignities she was obliged to suffer at Buffalero . . . where a room and female officers are appointed to undress and search Italian ladies'. Miss Sedgwick felt that travel in her own land would be 'somewhat diminished' if such regulations existed on the frontier between Pennsylvania and New York.[42]

Customs officers in England were no better. Allegations are made of indecent assault at Dover, and Miss Sedgwick thought her own experience at Portsmouth had been disgraceful: 'I felt it a mortification, as if the barbarism had been committed by my own kindred'.[43] Even T.N. Talfourd, a most vociferous opponent of the European system, had to admit that affairs in England were so bad they could only get better.[44] M.F. Tupper, a traveller of Talfourd's stamp, confessed our procedure at Folkestone was 'horrible and must ere long blow up; we are made quite ashamed of our country . . .; foreigners and unprotected females dread our coarse officials, whose politeness however is bribeable enough, if travellers would not be so stupid as to prefer having all their baggage ransacked before the loss of half-a-crown'.[45] The accolade of meanness, however, must go to Southampton where, as Henry Best recalled, an old lady was deprived of her pound of knitting but allowed to take the needles.[46]

If the above examples are centred on Europe, unhappy experiences at customs posts were nevertheless a worldwide misfortune. Forster tells of 'the dreaded attack of the custom-house officers' in eighteenth-century India: 'At the distance of every ten or twelve miles from Jumbo to the Chinnaun river, one of these petty tyrants takes his stand; and on the payment of a stipulated sum to the government, collects the public duties, as well as enforces every species of private exaction'.[47] It was no better in South America, where all the customs officials from Cape Horn to California were alleged to be in league with the smugglers. They were said to take bribes and inducements to eke out their miserable pay and connived at the export of specie, which was illegal beyond modest limits.[48]

There was little redress, after the event, for insults and corruption, but the astute and organized traveller kept his wallet and blood pressure in good condition by journeying with a minimum of immediate baggage. His large trunks or boxes could be carried separately by sea, arranged through the experience and wisdom of his travel agent. By travel agent is meant, before the era of Thomas Cook, the banker or merchant who arranged his credit. Many Grand Tourists had their heavy baggage sealed by the customs at Calais or Boulogne and dispatched via the Canal du Midi to Sète, the port for Montpellier. There, Ray & Co., expatriate English bankers, could arrange for its onward journey to Nice, Genoa, Leghorn, or even Florence. Smollett was a case in point.[49]

For those who chose to take their baggage with them, there was no shortage of hotel touts at ports of entry prepared to take charge of it. This could be an unnerving experience. At Antwerp are tales of elbowing porters and clamorous agents 'roaring out the names and properties of their own establishments, laying hold of your luggage, and nearly scratching your face with their cards'.[50] Cologne was particularly afflicted and its consistently bad reputation for touts culminated in Dod's attack on

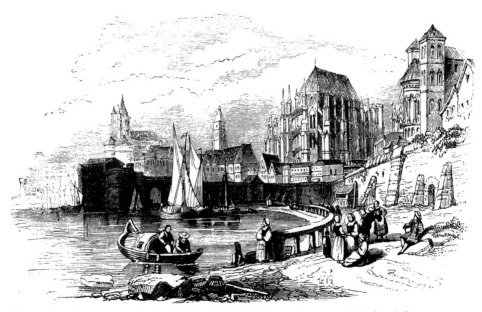

Cologne from the north, showing the cathedral choir in mid-picture. Begun in 1248, when Cologne was a powerful city in the Hanseatic League, the beautiful Gothic choir was the only part of the cathedral finished until a scheme to complete the building commenced in 1824

'the squalid wretchedness of the savage-looking, bustling crowds, who flew upon us when we landed on the quay' in 1820.[51] Coleridge's stanza, published a little later, springs to mind and it is easy to imagine that his own quayside arrival put him in such a startlingly savage mood about the city now famed for its toilet water:

> In Köhln, a town of monks and bones,
> And pavements fang'd with murderous stones,
> And rags, and hags, and hideous wenches,
> I counted two and seventy stenches,
> All well defined, and several stinks!
> Ye Nymphs that reign o'er sewers and sinks,
> The river Rhine, it is well known,
> Doth wash your city of Cologne;
> But tell me, Nymphs, what power divine
> Shall henceforth wash the river Rhine?[52]

In the world at large some travellers seem amazed at what could be done by trusting their belongings to well-proven corridors of freight. Our man in Havana is an example: rooked and harassed as described above, he felt the American mercantile house of Taylor & Co. was too good to be true. They promised to move his heavy baggage to North America without hitch but he had no confidence in their ability to do so. He was wrong, and repentant. 'The following morning [at New York] the first thing I did was to go to the merchants, Messrs Taylor and Co., to whom I had consigned my baggage . . ., and found that it had arrived safely. They charged me not a farthing for the trouble they must have taken in passing it through the custom-house, &c. Few persons would exercise such liberality.'[53]

The shipping of personal effects, with a minimum of fuss and expense, was also a by-product of colonization, and particularly of the military presence needed to perpetuate colonial authority. In the case of Britain, the pay, welfare, and provisioning of regiments was entrusted to civil agencies which were, or very soon became, private bankers. The best-known example was Cox & Co., established in the West End of London in 1758. During some 165 years of independent existence it gained great experience in shipping and forwarding. Having established its own branches in India, and later in Egypt, the firm became an obvious place where migrant civil servants and diplomats might also open an account. Any place in the world where British forces were sent was within the

The famous Cunard Steam Ship Co. Ltd (established in 1840 as the British & North American Royal Mail Steam Packet Co.) took its name from Samuel Cunard of Halifax, N.S., who held the British government's contract for carrying mail across the North Atlantic. It was one of several shipping lines later to issue its own traveller's cheques

bank's logistical reach. When Cox gave birth to its own travel agency (Cox & Kings (Agents) Ltd), there occurred again, as had happened with Thomas Cook & Co., a blurring of the boundaries between banking, forwarding and tourism.[54]

It only remains, as the story of travellers' money supply draws to its close, to find the real link between historical arrangements and the facilities of today. For although Robert Herries did the groundwork for paper credit in such a way that we can identify with his aspirations and techniques, it is to North America that the historian must look for the terminology and exact procedures with which we are now familiar. This means an enquiry must be made into the beginnings of transatlantic tourism and names must now be introduced which, although new in this study, are famous enough in the annals of banking and business, and sometimes in general knowledge.

Most Americans of the mid-nineteenth century who visited Britain did so under their own steam (metaphorically) and the idea of organized excursions came rather later than Thomas Cook's experiments in England. It was possible to sail from several East Coast ports to Glasgow and Liverpool, but the American Grand Tourist did best to catch a packet boat from New York, or from ports higher up the Hudson river, to disembark at Portsmouth, for London, or sail on to Le Havre. In later years, and into the Blue Riband era, liners sailed for Southampton, or if they were heading for the mainland of Europe they dropped passengers by tender at Plymouth, some five hours from London by steam train.

It was, however, on the Liverpool run that monetary provision arose. It was usual for prospective American travellers to open an account with Brown Brothers & Co., a mercantile house conveniently organized in New York, Boston, Philadelphia and Baltimore. This firm had its origins in the late eighteenth century when Alexander Brown, a Belfast linen merchant, emigrated to the New World. Three sons joined him in his East Coast offices while a fourth, William, opened a branch in Liverpool in 1810. With such strategic representation no one was better placed than the Brown family to augment the proceeds of commerce by the profits of leisure. The earliest record of this was in 1824 when a letter passed between the Baltimore and Liverpool houses establishing a credit for a John M. Colston of Virginia 'who crosses the Atlantic in search of Health & to see his Brother who resides in Paris'.[55]

In 1837 the Liverpool house, until then known as Messrs Wm. & James Brown, became Brown Shipley & Co.; a London office, by this title, was opened in 1863 and the Liverpool firm closed some twenty-five years later. The only form of money order used was the circular letter of credit, which could be issued in sterling to the intending traveller, while still in America, or could await him at Liverpool, or in later years at London, where he could also collect his mail. These instruments were, in essence, no different from those traditionally issued in Britain, except that the printed table of bankers formed an integral part of the document as a whole, which was endorsed on the back cover with a record of each withdrawal up to the ceiling and duration of the credit. The banker, whether in Harrogate or Hong Kong, reimbursed himself by a draft on Heywood, Kennard & Co., London (earlier Denison, Heywood & Kennard), who acted as bankers for Brown Shipley until, by their removal to London, they became bankers in their own right. For clarity of accounting, the draft bore the same serial number as the original letter of credit. Supplementary credits could be authorized in London or Liverpool by telegraph.[56]

In 1864 Brown Shipley opened a 'Travellers' Ledger' in Liverpool recording, under the customer's name and place of origin, credit arrangements authorized at the outset, or later, and details of withdrawals, taken from the drafts returned by correspondents. It is possible from this book to glimpse the travelling habits of middle-class Americans, mingling traditional European centres like Geneva, Venice and Frankfurt with Edinburgh, York and Leamington Spa.[57] Soon the small office of Brown Shipley in Founder's Court, near the Bank of England, became a kind of American clubhouse, where visitors sought the advice and resources of the firm which had become the financial agency for the United States government.

For evidence of organized excursions from America there is no better source than Mark Twain, who was involved at the beginning. His book *The Innocents Abroad*, often quoted above, is simply a record of his voyage on the SS *Quaker City* starting in New York City in February 1867 and embracing Europe, Asia Minor, the Holy Land, and North Africa. This was in every sense a new departure, and Twain prints the full text of the prospectus of the journey, leaving readers in no doubt as to the originality and excitement of the programme. 'For months the great Pleasure excursion to Europe and the Holy Land was chatted about in the newspapers everywhere in America, and discussed at countless firesides. It was a novelty in the way of Excursions – its like had not been thought of before, and it compelled that interest which attractive novelties always command.' The inclusive cost was $1,250, but travellers were recommended to take $5 a day in gold for other expenses.[58]

Few Americans, however, ventured abroad with only gold, and soon there was a useful alternative form of paper to the letter of credit. This was, of course, the so-called 'Traveler's Cheque', which first appeared in 1891. This form of credit was very much on the principle of Herries's circular note, but it is easy to see an all-American evolution, rather than a deliberate attempt to modify the European system. Few Americans would have been familiar with circular notes, as only letters of credit were issued by their own bankers, although in 1874 Thomas Cook had launched 'Circulating Notes' in New York under the general name of 'checks'. [59]

Praise for the introduction of this new instrument must be given to Marcellus Fleming Berry of the American Express Company. American Express began as an unincorporated concern in 1850. It was formed from a merger between three companies, all in the express delivery business, and its management brought together the famous names of Wells and Fargo. The early years saw rapid growth, but not without competition and another merger. The 1868 title of American Merchants Union Express Company was shortened to the modern form in 1873. James Congdell Fargo (1829–1915) became president in 1881 and under him came the introduction of the American Express money order in 1882 and then the traveller's cheque in 1891.[60]

The latter innovation followed a trip to Europe in 1890. Fargo found that letters of credit were 'no more use than wet wrapping paper' outside the urban centres, and Berry was asked to create a new kind of negotiable instrument with the acceptability of ready money. From their New York office at 65 Broadway, American Express controlled agencies in London, Liverpool, Paris and Bremen for promoting traveller's cheques. These were superseded by permanent branches in Paris, London (West End and City), Liverpool, Southampton, Bremen and Hamburg, while correspondent arrangements were formed with leading banks in France, Ireland (Dublin and Belfast), Scotland, Germany, Austria, Italy, Holland, Norway and Sweden. By an association with Credit Lyonnais, further outlets were gained at Brussels, Madrid, Geneva, Constantinople, Smyrna, Alexandria, Cairo and St Petersburg.[61]

Traveller's cheques were issued in denominations of $10, $20, $50 and $100 but could be exchanged in other money, equivalent values in sterling and other major currencies being printed on the document. The customer signed his traveller's cheques when he bought them and countersigned when he encashed them or made them payable to order. The advantage of this system to the traveller was flexibility, in that cheques need not even be presented through a bank, but could equally well be used as currency for the purchase of gifts and payment of services. One of the first traveller's cheques ever issued (see plate section) was cashed by a hotelier in Leipzig. There is evidence that circular notes had been usable in this way by the 1870s, but very much as a secondary role.[62] It was Herries's transferable exchange notes which were the real equivalent, but these had never been popular with the British and were phased out of use by the mid-nineteenth century.

Immediately, travellers' cheques were a success and widely copied. The American Bankers' Association (ABA) promoted their use among its members, underwritten by the Bankers' Trust Company of New York, established in 1903. The secretary to the trust, Thomas William Lamont (1870–1948), famous later as an international financier, travelled to Europe on behalf of the ABA to advertise their use.[63] In Britain, however, bankers tended to continue the promotion of circular notes and letters of credit in their advertising material, although issuing traveller's cheques themselves from the 1930s. It was the non-clearing banks with an obvious travel interest, like Thomas Cook & Son (Bankers) Ltd and the P. & O. Banking Corporation Ltd (established 1920) who first advertised traveller's cheques by name. Before the Second World War, however, clearing banks were issuing instructions to their staff to discourage the use of circular notes in favour of world letters of credit and traveller's cheques.[64]

The 1930s seemed quite rosy for the foreign traveller, especially the moneyed British. Sterling was in demand and restrictions were minimal. As the banking writer Norman Crump remembered, the tourist 'very often paid his hotel bill with an ordinary sterling cheque drawn on his home bank, just as if he were at Torquay or Bournemouth. If, when abroad, he ran short of money, he wrote or telegraphed home for more. On leaving home, he would cheerfully take a wad of British pound notes with him. . . . Alternatively, he would take a letter of credit, or traveller's cheques, . . . as much as he could afford or thought fit. In short, how much he spent on his holiday abroad was his business alone, and nobody else's'.[65]

This idyllic situation was, of course, blighted by the war. With the drain on reserves of international currencies, vigorous provisions were introduced by the Exchange Control Act 1947, to limit the export of British currency and restrict the spending capability of tourists outside the sterling area. The basic allowance for adults fluctuated according to pressures of politics and convertibility, being as low as £35, but rising to £100 in 1954–5; of this, £20 could be in foreign currency and the rest, normally, in traveller's cheques. Not until 1979, when the adult allowance had risen to £300, was exchange control abandoned and holiday money could be collected without the need to submit one's passport for annotation.

The most recent advances in banking technology have tended, ironically, to undermine the role of the traveller's cheque. A far wider acceptance of credit and charge cards abroad has made the tourist as flexible as his plastic friend. It is now more convenient for many people to settle payments by card and so gain a few weeks' credit before settling their account. It is also becoming increasingly popular abroad to draw out hard money against plastic, so one way or another the customary inter-bank agency and commission arrangements, based on the traditional encashment of paper, need to be under review.

This book has been something of a celebration of the traveller's cheque and it would be inappropriate to end with a kind of elegy on the prospect of its eventual demise. Let us compare it, rather, to a flower which has budded and bloomed through a glorious summer; but now the first little puckered petal warns that its life-span is finite.

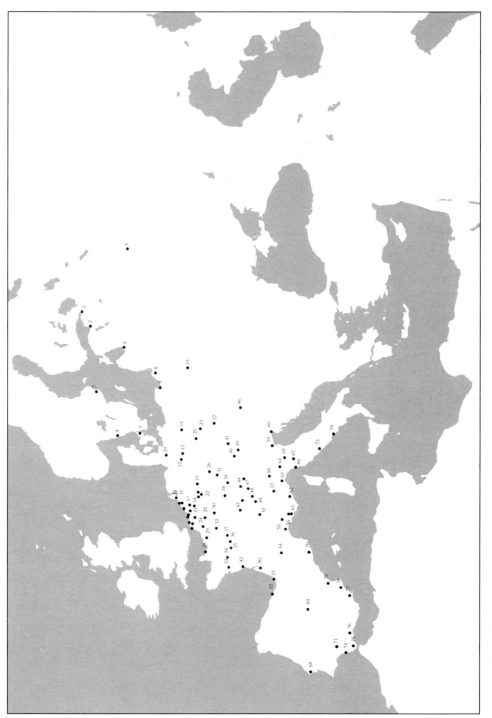

Location of Herries's Agencies 1769 (for key see opposite)

APPENDIX ONE

Maps showing locations of Herries's agencies in 1769 (beginning of scheme), 1795 (hey-day) and 1816 (after French Wars). (It has not been possible to name all locations on each map; every dot represents an agency and names are added as far as possible for orientation.)

1769: *91 outlets*

> The distribution shows clearly the influence of Robert Herries's formative years in the Low Countries and Spain, and the help he received from Messrs Hope & Co., the Amsterdam merchant-bankers. As a high proportion (more than one-third) of the outlets were in sea-ports – and some of these around the Baltic, and the pirate-infested waters between Cadiz and Barcelona – it appears that merchants as well as Grand Tourists were among Herries's intended clients.

1	St Petersburg	21	Lille	41	Ratisbon	61	Aix
2	Narva	22	Spa	42	La Rochelle	62	Nice
3	Stockholm	23	Dresden	43	Dijon	63	Genoa
4	Gothenburg	24	Amiens	44	Basel	64	Parma
5	Riga	25	St Quentin	45	Munich	65	Bologna
6	Moscow	26	Frankfurt	46	Vienna	66	Leghorn
7	Copenhagen	27	Prague	47	Berne	67	Florence
8	Königsberg	28	Caen	48	Lausanne	68	Lisbon
9	Danzig	29	Rouen	49	Geneva	69	Madrid
10	Hamburg	30	Rheims	50	Bordeaux	70	Barcelona
11	Amsterdam	31	Mannheim	51	Lyons	71	Seville
12	Hanover	32	Paris	52	Bilbao	72	Valencia
13	Brunswick	33	Nantes	53	Bayonne	73	Rome
14	Berlin	34	Angers	54	Toulouse	74	Cadiz
15	Warsaw	35	Tours	55	Montpellier	75	Gibraltar
16	Rotterdam	36	Blois	56	Avignon	76	Malaga
17	Antwerp	37	Orléans	57	Turin	77	Cartagena
18	Brussels	38	Nancy	58	Milan	78	Alicante
19	Cologne	39	Strasbourg	59	Venice	79	Naples
20	Leipzig	40	Augsburg	60	Trieste		

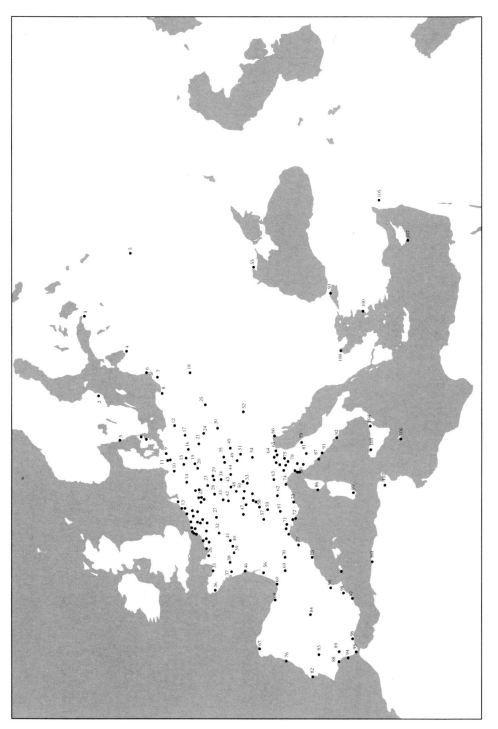

Location of Herries's Agencies 1795 (for key see opposite)

1795: *159 outlets*

At first sight there is little difference from 1769, but the density of outlets has increased considerably in a line from Germany through Switzerland to north Italy. Agencies have also now appeared in several Mediterranean islands and in European and Asian Turkey. Also in Asia, comes representation at Cherson (now Kherson) east of Odessa, and Aleppo in Syria. There are also outlets in two cities of North Africa (Algiers and Tunis). As more than one agency was now offered to travellers in Dresden, Frankfurt, Genoa, Hamburg, Leghorn, Milan and Naples, the number of outlets was actually increased by another eight.

1	St Petersburg	28	Trier	55	Kherson	82	Lisbon
2	Stockholm	29	Frankfurt	56	Bordeaux	83	Badajos
3	Gothenburg	30	Prague	57	Lyons	84	Madrid
4	Riga	31	St Malo	58	Geneva	85	Barcelona
5	Moscow	32	Paris	59	Chambéry	86	Ajaccio
6	Memel	33	Metz	60	Bayonne	87	Civita Vecchia
7	Königsberg	34	Mannheim	61	Avignon	88	San Lucar
8	Danzig	35	Nuremberg	62	Turin	89	Seville
9	Lübeck	36	L'Orient	63	Milan	90	Valencia
10	Bremen	37	Nantes	64	Vicenza	91	Rome
11	Hamburg	38	Angers	65	Venice	92	Naples
12	Stettin	39	Tours	66	Trieste	93	Constantinople
13	Rotterdam	40	Blois	67	La Coruña	94	Cadiz
14	Munster	41	Orléans	68	Bilbao	95	Gibraltar
15	Hanover	42	Nancy	69	Tarbes	96	Malaga
16	Magdeburg	43	Strasbourg	70	Toulouse	97	Cartagena
17	Berlin	44	Stuttgart	71	Nîmes	98	Alicante
18	Warsaw	45	Ratisbon	72	Aix	99	Cagliari
19	Göttingen	46	La Rochelle	73	Nice	100	Smyrna
20	Kassel	47	Dijon	74	Genoa	101	Algiers
21	Leipzig	48	Colmar	75	Bologna	102	Tunis
22	Spa	49	Augsburg	76	Oporto	103	Palermo
23	Cologne	50	Schaffhausen	77	Perpignan	104	Messina
24	Dresden	51	Munich	78	Lucca	105	Aleppo
25	Breslau	52	Vienna	79	Ancona	106	Valetta
26	Caen	53	Zürich	80	Siena	107	Cyprus
27	Rheims	54	Innsbruck	81	Florence	108	Salonika

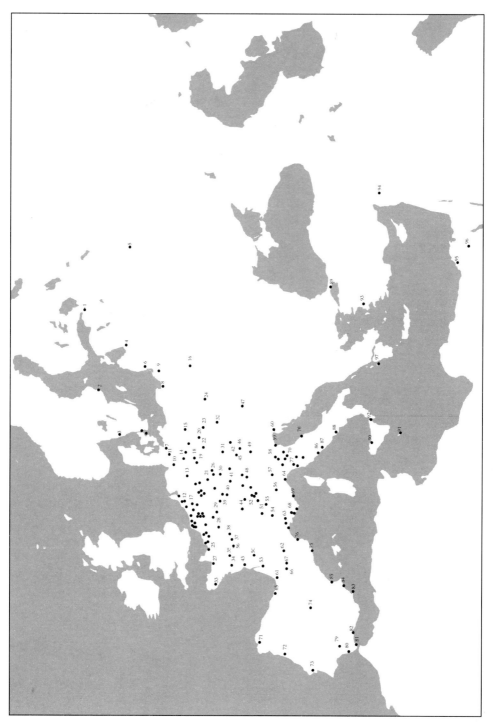

Location of Herries's Agencies 1816 (for key see opposite)

1816: *152 outlets*

A few new agencies have opened, but a greater number have closed. Algiers and Tunis (never great Grand Tourist destinations) have been replaced by Alexandria and Cairo. It is certain that many cities provided more than one agency, but the extent of duplication is unknown as no list of correspondents exists after the Napoleonic Wars.

Not long after this, once joint-stock banking had become established in Britain and elsewhere, it was virtually possible to present circular notes at any reputable foreign bank, and so lists of agencies tended to be discontinued, and maps of outlets became irrelevant.

1	St Petersburg	26	Frankfurt	51	Lyons	76	Perpignan
2	Stockholm	27	St Malo	52	Geneva	77	Florence
3	Gothenburg	28	Paris	53	Bordeaux	78	Ancona
4	Riga	29	Rheims	54	Tain	79	Seville
5	Moscow	30	Mannheim	55	Chambéry	80	Cadiz
6	Memel	31	Nuremberg	56	Turin	81	Gibraltar
7	Lübeck	32	Prague	57	Milan	82	Malaga
8	Danzig	33	L'Orient	58	Verona	83	Cartagena
9	Königsberg	34	Nantes	59	Venice	84	Alicante
10	Bremen	35	Angers	60	Trieste	85	Valencia
11	Hamburg	36	Tours	61	Bayonne	86	Civita Vecchia
12	Rotterdam	37	Blois	62	Toulouse	87	Rome
13	Münster	38	Orléans	63	Avignon	88	Naples
14	Brunswick	39	Nancy	64	Genoa	89	Constantinople
15	Berlin	40	Stuttgart	65	Bilbao	90	Palermo
16	Warsaw	41	Ansbach	66	Barèges	91	Valetta
17	Antwerp	42	Ratisbon	67	Bagnères	92	Messina
18	Magdeburg	43	La Rochelle	68	Aix	93	Smyrna
19	Kassel	44	Dijon	69	Nice	94	Aleppo
20	Leipzig	45	Augsburg	70	Lucca	95	Alexandria
21	Cologne	46	Munich	71	La Coruña	96	Cairo
22	Weimar	47	Vienna	72	Oporto	97	Zante
23	Dresden	48	Zürich	73	Lisbon		
24	Breslau	49	Innsbruck	74	Madrid		
25	Caen	50	Angoulême	75	Barcelona		

APPENDIX TWO

For over half the nineteenth century statistics are available of the numbers of circular and transferable notes issued to tourists and travellers by Herries, Farquhar & Co., at 16 St James's Street, London.

These graphs show how the issue of transferable notes fell away almost to nothing from the 1830s, in a very sudden decline. The issue of circular notes, on the other hand, mirrors the various political tensions affecting Europe, and particularly France, which discouraged continental travel. In 1830, for instance, Louis Philippe ousted Charles X, and Belgium broke away from Holland; while in 1848 there were general revolutionary movements throughout the Continent, and tourists did well to stay at home.

The relative decline in circular note issues from the 1850s reflects not so much a change in tourists' money supply as a lessening of Herries, Farquhar's share of the market.

HERRIES, FARQUHAR & COMPANY

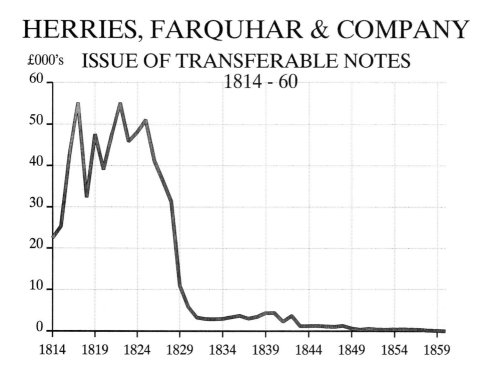

£000's   ISSUE OF TRANSFERABLE NOTES
1814 - 60

HERRIES, FARQUHAR & COMPANY

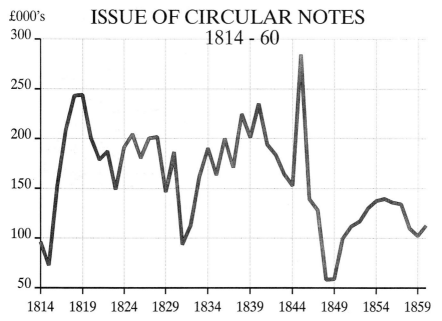

£000's   ISSUE OF CIRCULAR NOTES
1814 - 60

REFERENCES

For full titles of books, see Bibliography.
The following abbreviations are used:

BA: *Banking Almanac*
BEA: Bank of England Archives
BPP: *British Parliamentary Papers*
DNB: *Dictionary of National Biography*
EB: *Encyclopaedia Britannica*
JHC: *Journal of the House of Commons*
LBA: Lloyds Bank Archives
POA: Post Office Archives

CHAPTER ONE

1. Frith, pp. 281, 282
2. Maclean, pp. 68–71
3. [Tennent], vol. 1, pp. 240, 241
4. Dod, p. 89
5. Davis, p. 192
6. Croft, p. 121
7. Baster, pp. 3, 4
8. Aiton, pp. 22–4
9. Apart from Aiton, some of the fullest
    discussion of these matters is in Nugent,
    vol. 2, pp. 102–7, and Fortia de Piles,
    vol. 1, pp. 4–29
10. Clarke, vol. 9, pp. 22, 23
11. A useful introduction to bills of exchange is
    in Green, p. 16, etc
12. Train, p. 58
13. Macleod, vol. 2, p. 288; cf. Green, p. 13
14. Clarke, op. cit., p. 24
15. Fortia de Piles, vol. 4, p. 359
16. Zetzner ('Idylle Norvégienne'), pp. 56–8
17. See Fitzmaurice, p. 50
18. Zetzner ('Voyage . . . en Espagne'), p. 4
19. Thomas (ed.), vol. 2, p. 81
20. Smollett, p. 258
21. Wraxall, p. 23
22. Fortia de Piles, vol. 2, p. 2
23. Ibid., vol. 3, p. 103; Clarke, vol. 1, pp. xii,
    xiii
24. 'Russian paper money is not yet the worst
    in Europe.' Fortia de Piles, op. cit., pp. 102,
    103
25. Clarke, op. cit., p. 113
26. White, vol. 2, p. 71
27. Train, p. 20
28. Ibid., pp. 180, 181
29. Maxwell, p. 33

30. Eastlake (ed.), p. 220
31. Shelley (ed.), vol. 2, p. 147
32. Thomas (ed.), vol. 1, p. 321
33. Walsh, pp. 379, 380
34. *Voyages*, p. 46
35. Anderson (ed.), vol. 1, p. 169
36. Moryson, vol. 1, p. 70
37. W. Shakespeare, *The Merchant of Venice*, Act
    One, Scene Three
38. Mead, p. 174; Beattie, vol. 2, p. 262
39. Fortia de Piles, vol. 1, p. 260
40. Frith, p. 253
41. Terry, pp. 74, 75
42. Beckford, vol. 2, pp. 8, 9
43. Beattie, vol. 1, p. 144
44. Cochrane, vol. 2, p. 191
45. Tupper, p. 231
46. Brennan (ed.), p. 194
47. Anderson (ed.), vol. 1, p. 175
48. Dod, p. 93
49. Ibid., p. 91
50. Maxwell, p. 240, quoting Mrs F.E. King,
    A Tour in France, 1802 (1808), p. 77
51. Barrows (ed.), pp. 50, 51
52. Willis, p. 74
53. Smollett, p. 93
54. Best, pp. 210, 211
55. White, vol. 2, pp. 76, 77
56. Walsh, pp. 78, 79
57. Forster, vol. 2, p. 40
58. Train, p. 85
59. Campbell, vol. 1, p. 272
60. Vincent, p. 247
61. Train, p. 396
62. Frith, pp. 229, 230
63. Train, p. 429

CHAPTER TWO

1. *Recollections*, p. 119
2. Rye, p. 113, note 126
3. Babeau, p. 117
4. Moryson, vol. 2, p. 123
5. Howell, p. 28
6. Ibid., p. 28, 29
7. Moryson, op. cit., pp. 127, 128; Rye,
    p. xxiii, quoting from R. Dallington,
    Method for Travell (1598)
8. Moryson, op. cit., pp. 129, 130; Trease

(*Grand Tour*), p. 9; Bates, p. 344

9. Hodgskin, vol. 1, pp. 46, 47
10. Moryson, op. cit., p. 129
11. Smollett, p. 218
12. Walsh, p. 235
13. Thomas (ed.), vol. 2, p. 57
14. Forster, vol. 1, pp. 281, 282
15. Ibid., vol. 2, pp. 58, 73, 102
16. Reichard, p. i; Alison & Tytler, vol. 2, pp. 3, 4
17. Shelley, vol. 2, p. 32
18. Elliott, vol. 1, p. 200
19. Moryson, vol. 3, pp. 388, 402
20. Ibid., vol. 1, pp. 399, 400
21. Ibid., p. 79
22. Lambert (*Fortunate Traveller*), p. 44
23. [Tennent], vol. 1, pp. 83, 84
24. Moryson, vol. 2, p. 161
25. [Tennent], op. cit., p. 38
26. Matthews, p. 13
27. Trease (ed.), p. 113
28. Twain, p. 81
29. *Voyages*, p. 695
30. Howard, p. 95
31. Bacon, p. 55
32. 'Letters of recommendation not only to respectable bankers but also to various people in other walks of life, are or at least can be very useful. Do not slight this precaution.' Langlois, vol. 1, p. 30
33. *Recollections*, p. 16
34. Ibid., p. 205
35. Dod, p. 131
36. Brennan (ed.), p. 63
37. 'Do you want some schnaps, sir?' 'What is schnaps?' Walsh, p. 333
38. 'The universal use of French (only in polite society) seems to allow a Frenchman to know only his own language.' Fortia de Piles, vol. 1, p. v
39. Moryson, vol. 2, p. 59
40. Ibid.
41. Smollett, p. 115
42. Betham-Edwards (ed.), p. 276
43. Wraxall, p. 6
44. Thomas (ed.), vol. 2, p. 47
45. Kitchiner, vol. 1, p. 203
46. 'Judging by the lack of consideration from people whom one should be able to trust, one can guess what the rest are like.' Fortia de Piles, vol. 1, pp. 184, 185
47. Pückler-Muskau, vol. 3, pp. 36, 37
48. Barrows (ed.), p. 18
49. Anderson (ed.), vol. 1, p. 62
50. Ibid.
51. Eastlake (ed.), pp. 114, 115
52. 'Neither manufacturers, nor business men, nor even English people.' [Van Tets], pp. 165, 168, 169, 171, 173
53. Eastlake (ed.), pp. 132, 168
54. Ibid., pp. 228
55. Betham-Edwards (ed.), p. 128

56. Forster, vol. 2, p. 117; Train, p. 179
57. [Van Tets], p. 57
58. Walsh, pp. 332, 333
59. Forster, vol. 2, p. 36
60. Wraxall, p. 345
61. Ibid., p. 350
62. Tennant, vol. 1, pp. 327–31
63. Thomas (ed.), pp. 78, 84, 108
64. Smollett, p. 75
65. Ibid, p. 291

CHAPTER THREE

1. See *DNB sub* Sir Thomas Hope (d.1646) etc, and see Buist for more specialized and thorough history; also cf. Okey (ed.), p. 286: 'Mr Hope of Amsterdam, said to be the greatest merchant in the world . . .'
2. Forbes, p. 17
3. Ibid.
4. Ibid., p. 18; Sayers, p. 194
5. Forbes, p. 21
6. Ibid., p. 12; Healey, p. 83
7. Forbes, pp. 12,13; Healey, pp. 82, 83
8. Forbes, p. 18
9. Ibid., pp. 16, 21, 22; Healey, p. 88
10. Forbes, pp. 18, 19
11. Ibid. (introduction by Robert Chambers), p. iv; see also *DNB*
12. 'So strict was Mr John Coutts in discipline of the counting-house, that I slept but one night out of Edinburgh from . . . May 1754 till . . . September 1760, when I obtained leave to go to Aberdeenshire with my mother, to pay a visit to our relations.' Forbes, p. 14, footnote
13. Ibid., p. 22
14. Ibid., pp. 22, 23
15. Ibid., p. 23
16. Ibid., p. 28
17. LBA: A26b/3, f.2
18. Forbes, p. 29
19. Ibid.
20. Ibid.; Healey, p. 101
21. Forbes, p. 30. There is a circular, printed letter, unsigned but presumably issued by Herries, dated 24 Nov. 1769 (LBA: A26b/3, f.5) extolling the virtues of circular notes. This refers to '*Notre Maison à Edimbourg* (John Coutts & Co.)', as evidence of solidity. There are also items from October 1770. (cf. Sayers, p. 195, footnote 3)
22. Forbes, loc. cit.
23. Forbes, pp. 12, 15, 30
24. See note 21 above. Forbes, p. 30 (followed to a large extent by Healey, p. 101), gives the founding partners as Robert Herries, Robert Herries his uncle, Charles and William Herries his brothers, George Henderson, James Hunter, Forbes himself,

Mr. Pultney [*sic*], and Sir William Maxwell. This does not correspond with an original statement, 1 Oct. 1770, in LBA: A26b/4, f.3 but Henderson had a stake in the company from that date on

25. LBA: A26b/3, ff.1, 2, 46
26. LBA: A26b/3, f.6; A26b/4, f.2
27. Ibid., both undated documents. In the former (perhaps 1769) commission is stated as only half of one per cent, and it remained at that level for transferable notes
28. LBA: A26b/3, ff.39, 40 etc
29. e.g. 'Plan of Exchange Notes' (believed 1769), article 10 (LBA: A26b/3, f.1)
30. LBA: A26b/3, f.5 (page 2, para. 5)
31. LBA: A26b/3, ff.29, 30
32. 'Of a certain rank or reputation.' LBA: A26b/3, f.5 (p. 1, para. 6)
33. 'We do not intend, therefore, that you should make a fuss of our customers, or waste your time in entertaining them. They will be satisfied with your helpful manner and the normal business courtesies.' Ibid. (p. 5, para. 2)
34. LBA: A26b/3, f.2
35. Ibid.
36. Forbes, p. 31
37. Ibid., p. 33
38. Ibid., pp. 27, 28, 44–53. There is evidence of Herries's general unpopularity over the tobacco commission in Price, J.M. (ed.), p. 141. The London merchant Johnson called Herries & Co. [i.e. Robert Herries] 'damned rascals' in a letter of 1 June 1774: 'This stroke of theirs . . . to keep down the price is of the most villainous of acts. . . .'
39. Forbes, pp. 50, 51
40. Ibid., pp. 50, 53
41. LBA: A26b/4, f.18. He was on his way home 'from a Tour whose chief object was his own health'
42. LBA: A26b/3, f.14
43. Copy bond in LBA: Library Box 14. For kinship, see also P. Manning, *The Origins and Early History of Barclays Bank in Pall Mall* (London, 1985), p. 8; and Sayers, p. 198
44. Manning, op. cit., pp. 6, 8
45. LBA: A26b/3, f.21
46. LBA: A26b/5, f.3; A26b/4, ff.10, 14. Messrs Boyd, Ker & Co. of Paris also reimbursed agents for circular notes issued in Paris. Other refs in LBA: A26b/3, ff.32, 35
47. LBA: A26b/5, f.3; A26b/4, f.12
48. LBA: A26b/4, f.12
49. LBA: A26b/3, f.32
50. Ibid., f.35
51. LBA: A26b/4, ff.19, 20
52. LBA: A26b/3, f.36
53. LBA: A26b/4, f.21
54. LBA: A26b/5, f.3. This seems to mean 'a

kind of circulating bank' in as much as used circular notes, etc, were in constant travel from the periphery to the centre
55. '. . . since risks are always reduced by sharing them, while the objectives [of the business] increase for my successors'. Ibid.
56. Herries has a bad time in Healey where he is characterized as 'sharp, enterprising but ruthless' in his early years, and later 'an unscrupulous adventurer, capable of bribery' (p. 100). However, earlier historians of Coutts & Co. are inclined to be less harsh on Herries and more critical of the Coutts brothers (e.g. Coleridge, pp. 48, 49)
57. LBA: A26b/3, f.38 'Addenda'
58. LBA: A26b/4, f.13: '*Il est facheux que la Lettre d'ordre ait été perdue ou volée avec les Billets . . .* ' ('It is annoying that the Letter of Order was lost or stolen with the notes.')
59. Ibid., f.15
60. Lefevre, vol. 1, pp. 30–2
61. Aiton, p. 26
62. Matthews, p. 301
63. Sedgwick, vol. 1, pp. 165, 166
64. LBA: A26b/6
65. Ibid.; LBA: A26b/7
66. Reichard, p. i; Starke, p. 442
67. Reichard, loc. cit.; Maxwell, pp. 229, 230
68. Marchand (ed.), vol. 5, pp. 106, 107; vol. 10, pp. 135, 154
69. Holman, p. 51
70. Spencer, vol. 2, p. 363
71. Whitling, pp. 36, 37
72. LBA: Sayers's Ref. Files, No. 4199 (The original circular, apparently dated 18 Oct. 1815, has not survived.)
73. Aiton, p. 25
74. Campbell also refers (vol. 1, p. 3) to his 'circular letters' of Coutts & Co., 'carefully hidden in separate places according to orders'
75. Murray's *Handbook to Switzerland* (1874). Later editions warned of careless hoteliers not checking the Letter of Order
76. e.g. BEA: Birmingham Letter Books, C103/5, p. 292, 20 July 1841. A customer asked the best way to send money to her son, leaving for Malta. The Bank of England agent advised seven day accepted post bills
77. Campbell, vol. 1, p. 14
78. Aiton, pp. 27, 28
79. Weld, pp. 76–8
80. Spencer, vol. 2, p. 363
81. Aiton, p. 28
82. These countries were Austria, Finland, Rumania, Serbia, and Spain
83. Sayers, p. 198, quoting P. Sraffa (ed.), *The Works and Correspondence of David Ricardo*, vol. x (Cambridge, 1955), pp. 195, 223, 244, 341

84. LBA: A26b/3, f.47
85. Another prominent firm of Genevan bankers was Cazenove, Clavière et Fils (cf. Coulson, p. 31)
86. Roget, p. 96
87. Philips, p. 104
88. Marchand (ed.), vol. 5, pp. 93, 94, 107, 110, 112, 114, 118; vol. 8, p. 157; vol. 10, p. 228
89. Ibid., vol. 10, pp. 183, 228
90. Beckford, vol. 2, p. 82
91. [Best], pp. 82, 235, 236
92. Dod, p. 589
93. Sedgwick, vol. 1, pp. 162, 163
94. Howitt, p. 38
95. Sedgwick, vol. 1, p. 217
96. There is an excellent summary of Cook's achievements in Lambert (*Grand Tour*), chap. 8 (pp. 137–49)
97. Cook (*Dr W.H. Russell*), p. 60
98. cf. Brendon, p. 187, who gives figures for 1884 indicating that the Banking and Exchange Department of Thomas Cook & Son accounted for not much more than a third of the firm's profit
99. Cook (*Guide to . . . Excursions*), p. 13
100. Brendon, p. 163

CHAPTER FOUR

1. Piggott (ed.), p. 787
2. Hillaby (ed.), p. 138
3. e.g. Moritz, p. 32
4. Quarrell & Mare (eds), p. 124
5. Williams (ed.), p. 77
6. *Letters*, vol. 1, p. 82
7. Brennan (ed.), p. 27
8. Price, Valerie (ed.), pp. 90, 91
9. [Feldborg], vol. 1, pp. 185, 186
10. Acres, vol. 1, pp. 158, 159
11. LBA: A26b/3, ff.12, 13
12. Ibid., f.15
13. Ibid.
14. Ibid., f.16
15. LBA: A26b/4, f.8
16. Ibid.
17. LBA: A26b/3, f.16
18. Ibid.; A26b/4, f.8
19. LBA: A26b/4, f.9
20. POA: POST 96/20, Part 3, f.48
21. LBA: loc. cit.
22. LBA: A26b/5, f.2
23. e.g. LBA: A26b/3, f.22 (1786)
24. Ibid., f.26
25. LBA: A26b/4, f.11
26. Ibid., f.16
27. LBA: A26b/3, f.31
28. Robinson, pp. 102–6
29. LBA: A26b/3, f.31
30. LBA: A26b/4, f.16, postscript. For Palmer, see *DNB* and refs *passim* in Ellis, Lewins and Robinson

31. *BPP* (1829), ii, p. 347
32. LBA: A26b/3, f.16
33. LBA: A26b/4, f.11
34. One of the clearest summaries of the development of English banking is in Nevin & Davis, pp. 15–56
35. Fulford, pp. 246–55
36. Between 1750 and 1830 some 343 banking firms failed (Pressnell, p. 443)
37. Over seventy such indemnities have survived in the records of Moore & Robinson's Nottinghamshire Banking Company (LBA: A53/53b/8)
38. Robinson, pp. 98, 99
39. Ibid., pp. 97, 99, 136
40. Trench, pp. 1, 2
41. Brennan (ed.), pp. 28, 29
42. This constraint, introduced in 1708 (6 Anne, c.22, s.9), was not lifted until 1826, and even then remained in force within 65 miles of London until 1833
43. The annual publication *Bankers' Almanac* began listing banks and their branches in towns in 1845
44. 'A continuous nuisance.' Degrégny, pp. 103, 104
45. 'This feeling, no less than the fear of invasion, fosters opposition to a Channel tunnel.' Ibid., pp. 104, 105

CHAPTER FIVE

1. Howard, p. 3
2. Barrows (ed.), pp. 130, 131
3. Betham-Edwards (ed.), pp. 216, 217
4. Forster, vol. 2, pp. 8, 38–41
5. Ibid., pp. 41–3
6. Maxwell, p. 188
7. 33 Geo.III, c.4, ss.3,8; amended by 38 Geo.III, c.50
8. Lambert (*Fortunate Traveller*), p. 84; Spencer, vol. 2, pp. 361, 362
9. Reichard, pp. xiii, xiv; Whitling, p. 34. G. Chandler, in his history of Martin's Bank (*Four Centuries of Banking*, vol. 1 (London, 1964), p. 220) mentions confirmation given to the French ambassador in 1821 that a passport applicant 'has long been known to us and [we] believe him to be highly respectable'
10. Maclean, pp. 4, 9
11. Trease (ed.), p. 34
12. *BPP* (1852), xxviii, p. 545
13. Talfourd, p. 197
14. Tupper, p. 160
15. Wilkey, pp. 42, 43
16. Talfourd, pp. 4–6
17. *Recollections*, pp. 72, 158, 159, 234
18. Frith, p. 386
19. Twain, p. 7
20. Ibid., pp. 382, 383

21. Kiddy, pp. 154, 155
22. Moryson, vol. 1, p. 395
23. Ibid., vol. 2, pp. 74, 75
24. Elliott, vol. 1, pp. 353–6
25. White, vol. 2, pp. 77, 78
26. Walsh, pp. 234, 235
27. Willis, pp. 39, 40
28. Roberts, pp. 69, 70
29. [Feldborg], vol. 1, p. 65
30. *JHC*, vol. xcix (1844), p. 531
31. Twain, pp. 254, 308
32. Ibid., pp. 340–2
33. Graphically described in Walsh, vol. 1, pp. 216–25
34. Elliott, vol. 2, pp. 218, 220, 221
35. Maclean, pp. 269, 270
36. [Van Tets], pp. 13, 14
37. Barrows (ed.), p. 130
38. Spencer, vol. 1, p. 29
39. Ibid.
40. Tennant, vol. 1, pp. 195, 196
41. Roget, p. 161
42. Sedgwick, vol. 2, p. 25
43. Ibid., vol. 1, p. 137
44. Talfourd, pp. 240, 241
45. [Tupper], p. 253
46. [Best], p. 74
47. Forster, vol. 1, p. 347
48. *Recollections*, p. 91
49. Smollett, pp. 93, 106
50. [Aiton], p. 81
51. Dod, p. 552
52. Written in 1828; first published in 1834
53. *Recollections*, p. 309
54. Winton, pp. 21–5, and his research notes
55. BA (1890) [advert.]; Ellis, p. 130; Kouwenhoven, pp. 113, 114, 117. (Ellis and Kouwenhoven differ slightly in the wording of the letter re Colston.)
56. Ellis, pp. 95, 99, 130–8; Kouwenhoven, loc. cit.
57. The 'Travellers' Ledger' is in MSS Dept of the Guildhall Library, London (MS 20, 134)
58. Twain, pp. 1–5
59. *Achievement*, vol. 41, no. 5 (May, 1974), pp. 10, 11
60. *EB*, 15th ed. (1986), vol. 1, p. 328. Article 'Who started travellers cheques?' in *Westminster Review* (Feb. 1964), pp. 13, 14
61. BA (1899)
62. cf. Murray's *Handbook to Switzerland* (1874)
63. *EB*, ed. cit., vol. 7, pp. 123, 124 (*sub* Lamont, Thomas William)
64. In Lloyds Bank circular notes were discontinued in 1933. Letter from Chief Accountant to Colonial & Foreign Dept, 2 August 1933, states that 'for the past two years none has been issued as our customers, apparently, have preferred to use Travellers Cheques'
65. Crump, p. 289

BIBLIOGRAPHY

Acres, W. Marston, *The Bank of England from Within 1694–1900*, 2 vols (London, 1931)

[Aiton, J.], 'The Pedestrian', *Eight Weeks in Germany* (Edinburgh, 1842)

Alison, Sir A. & Tytler, A.F., *Travels in France 1814–15*, 2 vols (2nd ed., Edinburgh, 1816)

Almanach Royal

Babeau, A., *Les Voyageurs en France Depuis La Renaissance Jusqu'à La Révolution* (Paris, 1885)

[Bacon, F.], *The Essayes or Counsels Civill & Morall of Francis Bacon Lord Verulam* (Everyman, London, 1910)

Banking Almanac

Barrows, H. (ed.), *Hester Lynch Piozzi, Observations and Reflections Made in the Course of a Journey Through France, Italy, and Germany* (Ann Arbor, 1967)

Baster, A.S.J., *The Imperial Banks* (London, 1929)

Bates, E.S., *Touring in 1600* (London, 1911; republished Century, London, 1987)

Beattie, W., *Journal of a Residence in Germany . . . in 1822, 1825 & 1826*, 2 vols (London, 1831)

Beckford, P., *Familiar Letters from Italy, to a Friend in England*, 2 vols (London, 1805)

Best, H., *Four Years in France . . .* (London, 1826)

[Best, H.], *Italy as it is; or Narrative of an English Family's Residence for Three Years in that Country* (London, 1828)

Betham-Edwards, Miss (ed.), *Arthur Young's Travels in France . . . 1787, 1788, 1789* (London, 1892)

Black, J., *The British and the Grand Tour* (London, 1985)

Brackenhoffer, E., *Voyage de Paris en Italie 1644–1646* (Paris, 1927)

Brackenhoffer, E., *Voyage en France 1643–1644* (Paris, 1925)

Brendon, P., *Thomas Cook. 150 Years of Popular Tourism* (London, 1991)

Brennan, Flora (ed.), *Pückler's Progress* (London, 1987)

Browne, J.R, *An American Family in Germany* (New York, 1867)

Buist, M.G., *At Spes Non Fracta. Hope & Co. 1770–1815* (The Hague, 1974)

Campbell, J.F., *My Circular Notes*, 2 vols (London, 1876)

Carrington, Dorothy, *The Traveller's Eye* (London, 1947)

Clarke, E.D., *Travels in Various Countries of Europe Asia and Africa*, 11 vols (London, 1816–24)

Cobbett, J.P., *A Ride of Eight Hundred Miles in France* (London, 1824)

Cochrane, G., *Wanderings in Greece*, 2 vols (London, 1837)

Coleridge, E.H., *The Life of Thomas Coutts Banker* (London, 1920)

Cook, T., *Dr W.H. Russell of London, Consul Lever of Trieste and Cook's Tourists. Letters to his Royal Highness the Prince of Wales and to the Right Honourable the Earl of Clarendon, Foreign Secretary of State, In Reply to Various Misstatements and Calumnies . . .* (London, 1870)

Cook, T., *Guide to Cook's Excursions to Paris; and Directory of Excursions and Tours in Switzerland and Italy* (London & Leicester, [1865])

Corti, Count E.C., *The Rise of the House of Rothschild* (New York, [1972?])

Coryat[e], T., *Coryat's Crudities. Hastily gobled up in five Moneths travells in France, Savoy, Italie* (London, 1611; republished 2 vols, Glasgow, 1905)

Coulson, Mavis, *Southwards to Geneva* (Gloucester, 1988)

Croft, Pauline, *The Spanish Company* (London Record Society, 1973)

Crump, N., *The ABC of The Foreign Exchanges* (11th ed., London, 1951)

Davis, R., *Aleppo and Devonshire Square* (London, 1967)

Degrégny, J., *Londres* (Paris, 1888)

Dictionary of American Biography

Dictionary of National Biography

[Dod, C.E.], *An Autumn near the Rhine . . . in 1820* (2nd ed., London, 1821)

Eastlake, Lady (ed.), *Dr Rigby's Letters from France &c in 1789* (London, 1880)

Elliott, C.B., *Travels in the Three Great Empires of Austria, Russia and Turkey*, 2 vols (London, 1838)

Ellis, A., *Heir of Adventure. The Story of Brown, Shipley & Co. Merchant Bankers* (London, 1960)

Ellis, K., *The Post Office in the Eighteenth Century* (Oxford, 1969)

Encyclopaedia Britannica

[Feldborg, A.A.], 'J.A. Andersen', *A Dane's Excursions in Britain*, 2 vols (London, 1809)

Fitzmaurice, R.M., *British Banks and Banking. A Pictorial History* (Truro, 1975)

Forbes, Sir W., *Memoirs of a Banking-House* (London & Edinburgh, 1860)

Forster, G., *A Journey from Bengal to England . . .* , 2 vols (London, 1808)

Fortia de Piles, A.T.J. de, *Voyage de Deux Francais en Allemagne, Danemarck, Suéde, Russie et Pologne, Fait en 1790–1792*, 5 vols (Paris, 1796)

Frith, J., *Far and Wide. A Diary of Long and Distant Travel 1857–1860* (London, 1869)

Fulford, R., *Glyn's 1753–1953* (London, 1953)

Green, E., *Banking. An Illustrated History* (Oxford, 1989)

[Head, Sir F.B.], *Bubbles from the Brunnens of Nassau by an Old Man* (London, 1834)

Head, Sir F.B., *A Faggot of French Sticks*, 2 vols (London, 1852)

Healey, Edna, *Coutts & Co. 1692–1992. The Portrait of a Private Bank* (London, 1992)

Hibbert, C., *The Grand Tour* (London, 1987)

Hillaby, J. (ed.), *The Journeys of Celia Fiennes* (London, 1983)

Hilton Price, F.G., *A Handbook of London Bankers* (London, 1890–1)

Hodgskin, T., *Travels in the North of Germany*, 2 vols (Edinburgh, 1820)

Holman, J., *The Narrative of a Journey undertaken in the Years 1819, 1820 & 1821 . . .* (London, 1822)

Howard, Clare, *English Travellers of the Renaissance* (London, 1914)

Howell, J. *Instructions for Forreine Travell* (London, 1642) in Ed. Arber (ed.), *English Reprints* (London, 1869)

Howitt, W., *German Experiences . . .* (London, 1844)

Hyde, J.W., *The Post in Grant and Farm* (London, 1894)

Kiddy, J.G., *My Banker and I* (London, 1909)

Kitchiner, W., *The Traveller's Oracle; or, Maxims for Locomotion . . .* , 2 vols (London, 1827)

Kouwenhoven, J.A., *Partners in Banking. An Historical Portrait of a Great Private Bank. Brown Brothers Harriman & Co. 1818–1968* (New York, 1969)

Lambert, R.S. (ed.), *Grand Tour. A Journey in the Tracks of the Age of Aristocracy* (London, 1935)

Lambert, R.S., *The Fortunate Traveller* (London, 1950)

Langlois, H., *Itinéraire Complet du Royaume de France*, 2 vols (5th ed., Paris, 1824)

La Rochefoucauld, F., *Voyages en France, 1781–83*, 2 vols (Paris, 1933–8)

Leake, W.M., *Travels in the Morea*, 3 vols (London, 1830)

Lefevre, Sir G.W., *The Life of a Travelling Physician . . .* , 3 vols (London, 1843)

Letters from Albion to a Friend on the Continent, written in the Years 1810, 1811, 1812 & 1813, 2 vols (London, 1814)

Lewins, W., *Her Majesty's Mails: A History of the Post-Office* . . . (2nd ed., London, 1865)

Links, J.G., *Travellers in Europe* (London, 1980)

Londonderry, Marquis of, *Recollections of a Tour in the North of Europe in 1836–1837* (London, 1838)

Maclean, C., *An Excursion in France . . . from the Cessation of Hostilities in 1801, to the 13th of December 1803* . . . (London, 1804)

Macleod, H.D., *The Theory and Practice of Banking*, 2 vols (London, 1866)

Marchand, Leslie A. (ed.), *Byron's Letters and Journals 1816–1823*, 12 vols (London, 1973–82)

Matthews, H., *The Diary of an Invalid. Being the Journal of a Tour in Pursuit of Health . . . in . . . 1817, 1818, 1819* (2nd ed., London, 1820)

Maxwell, Constantia, *The English Traveller in France 1698–1815* (London, 1932)

Mead, W.E., *The Grand Tour in the Eighteenth Century* (Boston & New York, 1914)

Moritz, C.P., *Journeys of a German in England in 1782* (London, 1965) [also, *Travels of Carl Philipp Moritz in England in 1782* (London, 1924), a reprint of English translation of 1795]

Moryson, F., *An Itinerary Containing His Ten Yeeres Travell, etc*, 4 vols (London, 1617, republished Glasgow, 1907–8)

Nevin, E. & Davis, E.W., *The London Clearing Banks* (London, 1970)

Nugent, T., *The Grand Tour containing an exact description of most of the Cities, Towns and Remarkable Places of Europe*, 4 vols (London, 1749)

Okey, T. (ed.), *Travels in France & Italy During the Years 1787, 1788 and 1789 by Arthur Young* (Everyman, London, 1927)

Oldmixon, J., *Gleanings from Piccadilly to Pera* (London, 1854)

Philips, H., *Continental Travel in 1802–3. The Story of an Escape* (Manchester, 1904)

Piggott, S. (ed.), *Camden's Britannia: Facsimile of 1695 Edition published by Edmund Gibson* (Newton Abbot, 1971)

Pressnell, L.S., *Country Banking in the Industrial Revolution* (Oxford, 1956)

Price, J.M. (ed.), *Joshua Johnson's Letterbook, 1771–1774* (London Record Society, 1979)

Price, Valerie (ed.), *A Frenchman Sees the English in the 'Fifties* (London, 1935)

Pückler-Muskau, H.L.H., *Tour in Germany, Holland and England in the Years 1826, 1827 & 1828*, 4 vols (London, 1832)

Pudney, J.S., *The Thomas Cook Story* (London, 1953)

Quarell, W.H. & Mare, M. (eds), *London in 1710 from the Travels of Zacharias Conrad von Uffenbach* (London, 1934)

Rae, W.F., *The Business of Travel. A Fifty Years' Record of Progress* [Thomas Cook & Son] (London, 1891)

Raffles, T., *Letters during a Tour through some Parts of France, etc. . . . in 1817* (Liverpool, 1820)

Recollections of a Ramble from Sydney to Southampton (London, 1851)

Reichard, M., *An Itinerary of France and Belgium; or, The Traveller's Guide . . .* (London, 1822)

Roberts, Emma, *Notes of an Overland Journey through France and Egypt to Bombay* (London, 1841)

Robinson, H., *Britain's Post Office* (Oxford, 1953)

Roget, S.R., *Travel in the Two Last Centuries of Three Generations* (London, 1921)

Russell, J., *A Tour in Germany . . . in the Years 1820, 1821, 1822*, 2 vols (2nd ed., Edinburgh, 1825)

Rye, W.B., *England as Seen by Foreigners in the Days of Elizabeth and James the First . . .* (London, 1865)

Sayers, R.S., *Lloyds Bank in the History of English Banking* (Oxford, 1957)

Sedgwick, Miss, *Letters from Abroad to Kindred at Home*, 2 vols (London, 1841)

Shelley, Mrs. (ed.), *Essays, Letters from Abroad . . . By Percy Bysshe Shelley*, 2 vols (London, 1840)

Sherer, J.M., *Notes and Reflections During a Ramble in Germany* (London, 1826)

Smollett, T., *Travels through France and Italy* (London, 1907)

[Spencer, E.], *Sketches of Germany and the Germans, with a glance at Poland, Hungary, & Switzerland in 1834, 1835, and 1836*, 2 vols (London, 1836)

Starke, M., *Information and Directions for Travellers on the Continent* (6th ed., London, 1828)

Stokes, M. Veronica, *A Bank in Four Centuries* [Coutts], (London, 1978)

Stoye, J.W., *English Travellers Abroad 1604–1667* (London, 1952)

Svedenstierna's Tour of Great Britain 1802–3 (Newton Abbot, 1973)

Swan, The Revd C., *Journal of a Voyage up the Mediterranean . . .* 2 vols (London, 1826)

Swinglehurst, E., *Cook's Tours: The Story of Popular Travel* (Poole, [1982])

Talfourd, T.N., *Vacation Rambles and Thoughts . . . in the Vacations of 1841, 1842, and 1843* (London, 1845)

Tennant, C., *A Tour through Parts of the Netherlands, Holland, Germany, Switzerland, Savoy, and France, in the Year 1821–2*, 2 vols (London, 1824)

[Tennent, J.E.], 'J. Emerson', *Letters from the Aegean*, 2 vols (London, 1829)

Terry, C., *Scenes and Thoughts in Foreign Lands* (London, 1848)

Thomas, W.M. (ed.), *The Letters and Works of Lady Mary Wortley Montagu, edited by her Great-Grandson Lord Wharncliffe*, 2 vols (London, 1861)

Thomson, W., *Dictionary of Banking* (London, 1911) [many other editions]

Train, G.F., *Young America Abroad* (London, 1857)

Trease, G., *The Grand Tour* (London, 1967)

Trease, G. (ed.), *Matthew Todd's Journal* (London, 1968)

[Trench, Mrs. R.], *Journal Kept During a Visit to Germany in 1799, 1800* (London, 1861)

[Tupper, M.F.], *Paterfamilias's Diary of Everybody's Tour* (London, 1856)

Twain, M. [Samuel L. Clemens], *The Innocents Abroad, or The New Pilgrims' Progress* (Hartford, 1875)

[Van Tets, Henrica. R.], *Voyage D'Une Hollandaise en France en 1819* (Paris, 1966)

Vincent, Mrs H., *Forty Thousand Miles over Land and Water* (London, 1886)

Voyages and Travels of her Majesty Caroline Queen of Great Britain . . . (London, 1821)

Walsh, The Revd R., *Narrative of a Journey from Constantinople to England* (3rd ed., London, 1829)

Weld, C.R., *Auvergne, Piedmont, and Savoy* (London, 1850)

White, C., *Three Years in Constantinople . . .*, 3 vols (London, 1845)

[Whitling, H.J.], 'Nil', *Heidelberg and The Way Thither* (London, 1845)

Wilkey, E., *Wanderings in Germany . . .* (London, 1839)

Williams, Clare (ed.), *Thomas Platter's Travels in England 1599* (London, 1937)

Willis, N.P., *Pencillings by the Way* (New York, 1844)

Winton, J.R., *Lloyds Bank 1918–1969* (Oxford, 1982)

Wood, A.C., *A History of the Levant Company* (Oxford, 1935)

Wraxall, N.W., *A Tour Round the Baltic, Thro' the Northern Countries of Europe . . .* (4th ed., London, 1807)

Zetzner, J.E., 'Idylle Norvégienne d'un Jeune Négociant Strasbourgeois'; 'Londres et l'Angleterre en 1700'; and 'Un Voyage d'Affaires en Espagne en 1718', all republished in *Revue d'Alsace* (1905–7)

INDEX